An Atlas of Investigation and Diagnosis

ALZHEIMER'S DISEASE

Daniel W McKeel, Jr
Alzheimer's Disease Research Center
Washington University School of Medicine
St Louis, Missouri, USA

Jeffrey M Burns
Alzheimer and Memory Program
University of Kansas School of Medicine
Kansas City, Kansas, USA

Thomas M Meuser
Alzheimer's Disease Research Center
Washington University School of Medicine
St Louis, Missouri, USA

John C Morris
Alzheimer's Disease Research Center
Washington University School of Medicine
St Louis, Missouri, USA

CLINICAL PUBLISHING

OXFORD

Clinical Publishing
an imprint of Atlas Medical Publishing Ltd
Oxford Centre for Innovation
Mill Street, Oxford OX2 0JX, UK

Tel: +44 1865 811116
Fax: +44 1865 251550
Email: info@clinicalpublishing.co.uk
Web: www.clinicalpublishing.co.uk

A catalogue record of this book is available from the British Library

ISBN-13 978-1-84692-30-1
ISBN-10 1-84692-30-2

The publisher makes no representation, express or implied, that the dosages in this book are correct. Readers must therefore always check the product information and clinical procedures with the most up-to-date published product information and data sheets provided by the manufacturers and the most recent codes of conduct and safety regulations. The authors and the publisher do not accept any liability for any errors in the text or for the misuse or misapplication of material in this work.

Printed by T G Hostench SA, Barcelona, Spain

Contents

Preface

Knowledge about the clinical, neuropsychological, neuro-imaging, biochemical, molecular, and neuropathological characterization of neurodegenerative dementing disorders is rapidly growing. This atlas was conceived as a compendium of clinical and neuropathological descriptions of these features and is intended to inform all who are interested in the dementing disorders, including students, postdoctoral trainees, health care professionals, practicing physicians, and scientists. The emphasis is on clinical and pathological differential diagnosis.

This atlas is not meant to be a comprehensive treatise but rather a focused review that can be used to gain a rapid and up-to-date perspective on key features of dementing neuro-degenerative disorders. The neuroimaging and pathologic illustrations and the literature citations in each chapter are selected to enhance the reader's understanding of disease expression and differential diagnostic features. We include both seminal and recent references with preference being given to reviews. We believe in establishing reliable clinico-pathological relationships that assist in arriving at an accurate final diagnosis as a critical element in the effort to assess new treatments and in presenting new research findings.

Each chapter includes summary tables of core clinical and neuropathologic features of the disease or disease family being discussed. An exhaustive coverage of each topic is beyond the scope of this monograph; several excellent books cover specific topics in more depth.

The atlas was authored by clinician-scientists from the Alzheimer's Disease Research Center (ADRC) at Washington University in St Louis, Missouri, and at the University of Kansas School of Medicine, in Kansas City, Kansas, USA. As such, it reflects the contributions of our many colleagues and collaborators who have influenced us in numerous important ways. Chief among these influences

is the ADRC's focus in the clinical distinction of early-stage dementia from nondemented aging by eliciting evidence of intraindividual cognitive decline from previously attained levels and on the validation of these distinctions through clinicopathological correlations.

Chapter 1 is a clinical overview of dementing disorders. The diagnosis of these disorders focuses on Alzheimer's disease (AD) because it is by far the most common cause of dementia in older adults. The growing role of neuroimaging in clinical settings and in research is also discussed.

Chapter 2 presents an approach to the behavioral assessment of AD dementia with neuropsychological tests.

Chapter 3 addresses autopsy and histopathological methods used in the ADRC's Neuropathology Core to diagnose various adult dementias in over 1,050 brains from longitudinally characterized research subjects. Routine histopathologic, special dye and silver stains, and immunohistochemical techniques as well as specialized autopsy techniques for brain, cerebrospinal fluid, and pituitary gland removal are presented and illustrated. Selected staining protocols used in the ADRC Neuropathology Core laboratory are presented in the Appendix.

Chapter 4 covers the spectrum of aging-associated neuropathologic findings that form the necessary baseline for assessing abnormalities caused by dementing disorders. Even today, our knowledge base of these important features of healthy or 'normal' brain aging are incompletely defined.

Chapter 5 focuses on the neuropathology of AD. Our research indicates that AD pathology may begin in the sixth decade of life or even earlier with focal deposition of preamyloid and diffuse beta amyloid plaques, accompanied by very focal formation of pretangles and tangles in certain specific cerebral regions. The lesion profiles are associated with very mild, mild, moderate, and severe dementia as defined by the Clinical Dementia Rating (CDR), which was developed in 1982 by Leonard Berg, Charles Hughes, and colleagues at the predecessor to our ADRC and was updated by John C Morris in 1993. The chapter also discusses the roles of vascular disease and cerebral amyloid angiopathy and cerebrovascular lesions as they interact with other features of AD pathology.

We acknowledge with gratitude the large team of physicians in several specialties, nurses, psychologists, basic scientists, and others who make the ADRC a wonderfully stimulating environment in which to work and ultimately have made this book possible. We also are indebted to our research participants and their families who unstintingly give their time and support to the ADRC's efforts to conquer the dementing illnesses. The ADRC and its affiliated research programs have been supported for over two decades by the National Institute on Aging (Bethesda, Maryland), primarily through grants P01 AG03991 and P50 AG05681. Finally, we dedicate this atlas to our spouses, Louise, Jennifer, Christy, and Lucy, whose support makes our work possible.

Daniel W McKeel, Jr, MD
Jeffrey M Burns, MD
Thomas M Meuser, PhD
John C Morris, MD

This book is derived from:
Dementia: an Atlas of Investigation and Diagnosis
ed DW McKeel Jr, JM Burns, TM Meuser, JC Morris
Oxford 2007 Clinical Publishing
ISBN 978 1 904392 37 8

Abbreviations

A4 amyloid beta peptide (synonyms a-beta, Aβ, BAP, 4 kd protein)

AAN American Academy of Neurology

AANP American Association of Neuro-pathologists

ACTH adrenocorticotropic hormone

AD Alzheimer's disease

ADL activities of daily living

ADRC Alzheimer's Disease Research Center

ADRDA Alzheimer's Disease and Related Disorders Association

AGD argyrophilic grain disease

ALS amyotrophic lateral sclerosis

AON anterior olfactory nucleus

apoE apolipoprotein E

APP amyloid precursor protein

aSYN alpha-synuclein

BCRS Brief Cognitive Rating Scale

CA corpora amylacea

CAA cerebral amyloid (a-beta) angiopathy

CC corpus callosum

CDR Clinical Dementia Rating

CERAD Consortium to Establish a Registry for Alzheimer's Disease

CLB cortical Lewy body

CNS central nervous system

CP choroid plexus

CR Congo red

(pm)CSF (postmortem) cerebrospinal fluid

CT computed tomography

DAB diaminobenzidine (stain)

DAT dementia of Alzheimer's type

DG Dentate gyrus

DH2O distilled water

DIC differential interference contrast

DLB dementia with Lewy bodies

DLDH dementia lacking distinctive histopathology

DN dystrophic neurite

DR dorsal raphe

DS Down's syndrome

DSM Diagnostic and Statistical Manual

DSP diffuse senile plaque

EEG electroencephalogram

EM electron microscopy

ERC-II entorhinal cortex layer II stellate cells

FFPE formalin-fixed paraffin-embedded

fMRI functional magnetic resonance imaging

FTD frontotemporal dementia

GCI glial cell inclusions

GDS Global Deterioration Scale

GFAP glial fibrillary acidic protein

GP-COG General Practitioner Assessment of Cognition

GVD granulovacuolar degeneration

H&E hematoxylin eosin (stain)

HIPAA Health Insurance Portability and Accountability Act

ICA internal carotid artery

IHC immunohistochemistry

IQCODE Informant Questionnaire on Cognitive Decline in the Elderly

IRB Institutional Review Board

LB Lewy body

LC locus ceruleus

LFB luxol fast blue

LN Lewy neurite

LP lumbar puncture

mab monoclonal antibody

MCI mild cognitive impairment

MMSE Mini-mental State Examination

MND motor neuron disease

MRI magnetic resonance imaging

mRNA messenger ribonucleic acid

MSA multiple system atrophy

NACC National Alzheimer Coordinating Center, Seattle, WA, USA

NBF neutral buffered formalin

NBM nucleus basalis of Meynert

NFP neurofibrillary pathology

NFT neurofibrillary tangle

NIA National Institute on Aging

NINCDS-ADRDA National Institute of Neurologic and Communicative Disorders and Stroke and the Alzheimer's Disease and Related Disorders Association

NNSP non-neuritic senile plaque

NSP neuritic senile plaque

NT neuropil thread

PAS periodic acid-Schiff

PD Parkinson's disease

PET positron emission tomography

PHF paired helical filaments

PHF tau hyperphosphorylated tau

PIB Pittsburgh compound-B

PMI postmortem interval

PP perforant pathway

PS1(2) presenilin 1(2)

PSFF paraffin sections of formalin fixed

PSP progressive supranuclear palsy

SBT Short Blessed Test

SGL supragranular layer

SN substantia nigra

SP senile plaque

SPECT single photon emission computed tomography

TIA transient ischemic attack

TSH thyroid stimulating hormone

TSP total senile plaques

VaD vascular dementia

WM white matter

WML white matter lesion

Chapter 1

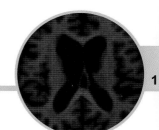

Cognitive aging and dementia: an overview

Introduction

In 1907 Alois Alzheimer first described the clinical and pathologic features of the disease that now bears his name. Professor Alzheimer was among the first to correlate higher order cognitive dysfunction with changes in brain structure. Since then, the science of neuropathology has played an important role in the nosology of dementia, as Professor Alzheimer predicted:

'It is clear that there exist many more mental diseases than our textbooks indicate. In many such cases, a further histological examination must be effected to determine the characteristics of each single case. We must reach the stage in which the vast well-known disease groups must be subdivided into many smaller groups, each with its own clinical and anatomical characteristics' (translation by Bick & Amaducci, 1989).

Our understanding of disorders of higher cognitive function has advanced considerably in the last century, largely as a result of clinicopathologic studies such as Professor Alzheimer's. While molecular genetics and DNA analysis are now contributing importantly to disease classification, clinical and pathologic classifications will remain essential to interpreting the relationship of genotype and phenotype (Morris, 2000).

Dementia

Dementia is a clinical syndrome of acquired cognitive impairment produced by brain dysfunction. Dementia represents a decline from a higher level of cognitive function such that accustomed activities are accomplished less well or relinquished altogether. The American Academy of Neurology recommends the routine use of the Diagnostic and Statistical Manual (DSM) criteria for diagnosing dementia, which has been shown to be a reliable indicator of the presence of dementia (*Table 1.1*).

Dementia is a common disorder in older adults, involving as many as 10% of those over the age of 65 years. Increased life expectancy in the US and other developed countries has fueled an unprecedented growth in the elderly population

---

Table 1.1 Definition of dementia: DSM IV

- Impairment in short- and long-term memory, associated with impairment in abstract thinking, impaired judgment, other disturbances of higher cortical function, or personality change
- The disturbance is severe enough to interfere significantly with work or usual social activities or relationships with others

(American Psychiatric Association, 1994)

that is leading to dramatic increases in the incidence of dementia. The prevalence of the most common cause of dementia, Alzheimer's disease (AD), doubles every 5 years after the age of 65 years, and reaches nearly 50% after age 85 years (Evans *et al.*, 1989) (**1.1**). Currently, there are an estimated 4.5 million people in the US with AD and 20 million worldwide (World Health Organization); the incidence of AD has been projected to nearly triple in the US over the next 50 years (Hebert *et al.*, 2001) (**1.2**). The annual treatment costs of AD in the US are estimated at $100 billion with the cost to government agencies rising rapidly: Medicare spending on AD will grow to $49.3 billion (a 54% increase over the costs in 2000), and Medicaid spending will grow to $33 billion (an 80% increase over costs in 2000) (Prigerson, 2003).

Brain aging and dementia

It is well accepted that advancing age is associated with cognitive changes. When compared directly with younger subjects, older subjects tend to process information at a slower rate, manipulate and store information (working memory) less efficiently, and have declines in free-recall of word lists. On the other hand, cognitive declines with age are not universal to all types of cognition. For instance, crystallized intelligence (such as measures of knowledge and vocabulary) is stable across the lifespan (Park *et al.*, 2001) (**1.3**). Additionally, the magnitude of the deficits observed with age generally are small and do not appear to impair overall function appreciably or the ability to carry out activities of daily living (Rubin *et al.*, 1993).

The aging brain is associated with structural changes in even the healthiest individuals that may underlie some of the cognitive changes that are observed with age. Normal aging is associated with a slow and steady loss of brain tissue beginning in early adulthood and continuing over the lifespan (**1.4**) (Jernigan *et al.*, 2001; Bartzokis *et al.*, 2003; Fotenos *et al.*, 2005). White matter myelination continues into the fourth decade (Hildebrand *et al.*, 1993; Bartzokis *et al.*, 2001) but declines thereafter, with the occurrence of

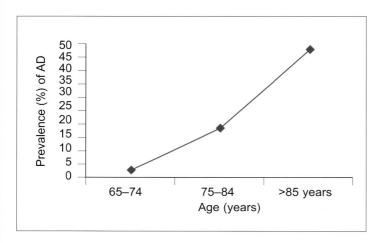

1.1 Prevalence of Alzheimer's disease in an aging population. Prevalence increases dramatically with age and approaches 50% of those over 85 years old. (Adapted from Evans *et al.*, 1989.)

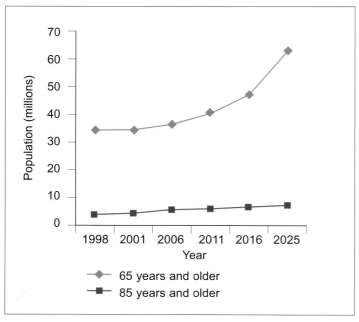

1.2 Population estimate for older adults in the US. The US Census Bureau (2000) projects the population of 65 years will increase dramatically by the year 2025 (middle series estimates). The 85 years and older group is the fastest growing segment of the population.

normal age-related breakdown in myelin (**1.5**) and the accumulation of changes in the white matter on magnetic resonance imaging (MRI) in older adults (**1.6**) (Longstreth *et al.*, 1996). Subclinical or 'silent' brain infarcts are present in up to 33% of nondemented older adults (Longstreth *et al.*, 1996; Vermeer *et al.*, 2002) and increase in prevalence with increasing age. These age-related brain changes are likely to play a role in the changes in cognition that occur

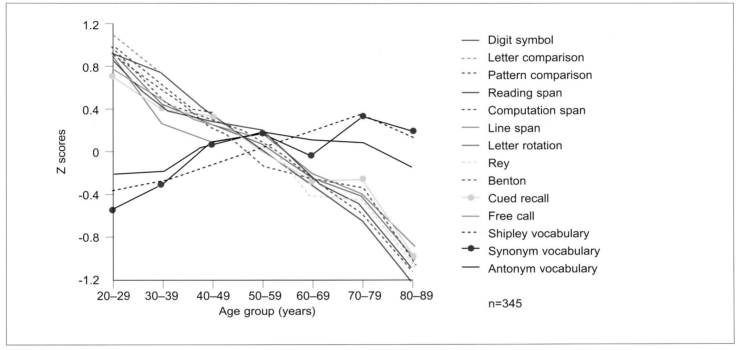

1.3 Cognitive decline with age. Some aspects of cognition, such as processing speed and working memory, are consistently reported to decline with age while others such as vocabulary, remain stable. Methodologic issues complicate these findings as longitudinal studies (following one individual over time) show less or no decline in cognition than cross-sectional studies (groups of individuals studied at one point in time). (Adapted from Park *et al.*, 2001.)

1.4 Cross-sectional plot of brain volume across the adult lifespan. Normal aging is associated in a slow and steady loss of brain tissue beginning in the seventh decade and extending over the lifespan. DAT: dementia of Alzheimer type; nWBV: normalized whole brain volume. (Adapted from Fotenos *et al.*, 2005.)

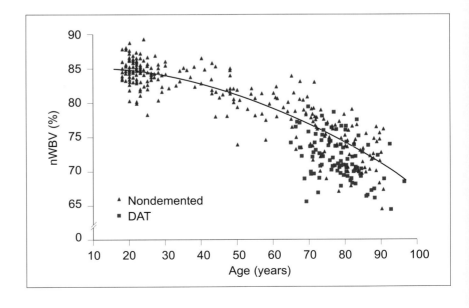

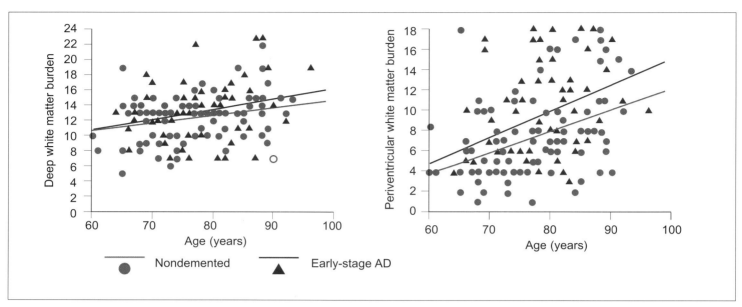

1.5 The burden of white matter lesions increases with age in individuals with early stage AD and healthy controls. (Adapted from Burns *et al*., 2005.)

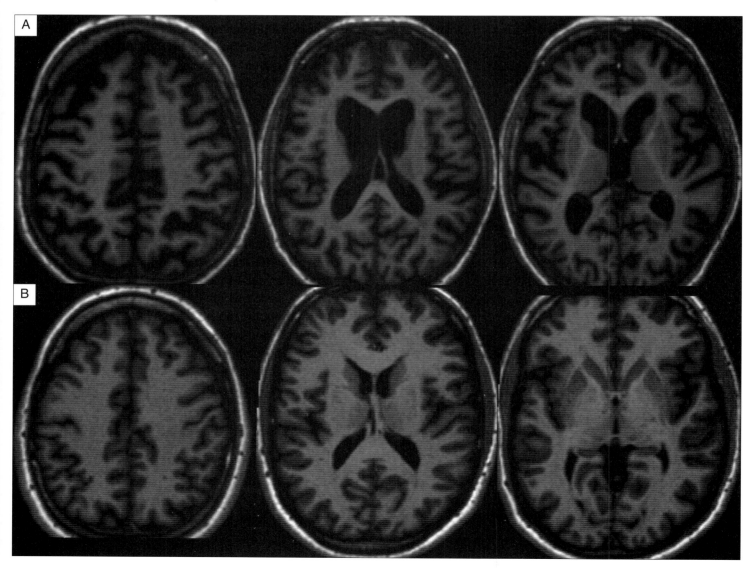

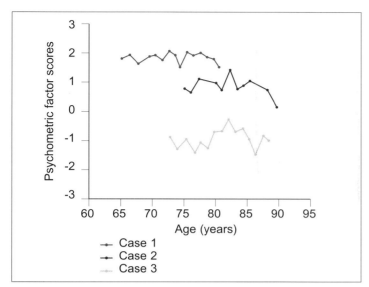

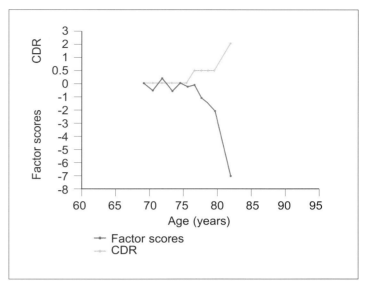

1.7 Stable cognitive performance with age in three nondemented controls. Factor score is an index of general cognitive performance generated from a battery of neuropsychologic tests. The large majority of a group of nondemented subjects followed for up to 15 years showed no decline in a standardized score of general cognitive performance.

1.8 Cognitive decline in dementia. An abrupt decline in psychometric performance (green) occurs in this individual once subtle cognitive decline is detected (Clinical Dementia Rating (CDR) of 0.5, yellow). Stable cognitive performance is generally maintained up until the onset of a dementing illness, at which time a steep decline in performance occurs. Factor score is an index of cognitive performance. (Adapted from Rubin *et al.*, 1998.)

with advancing age. Additionally, there is a complex relationship between age-related brain changes and AD pathology. For instance, less AD neuropathology is required to produce clinically apparent dementia in the setting of cerebrovascular disease (Snowdon *et al.*, 1997; Esiri *et al.*, 1999; Zekry *et al.*, 2002). Thus, age-related brain changes are likely to contribute to the cognitive changes seen in healthy aging but also appear to influence the expression of AD in the aging population.

A central but unresolved issue is determining which cognitive changes can be accepted as part of normal aging. The mildest cognitive changes ascribed to early AD overlap considerably with cognitive performance in healthy aging

1.6 (Opposite.) Brain atrophy with age. Global atrophy is apparent in the brain of a 90-year-old nondemented man (**A**). The ventricles are significantly enlarged with prominent sulci. For comparison, a 39-year-old nondemented man (**B**) demonstrating smaller ventricles, fuller white matter, and less prominent sulci. (Courtesy of Randy L Buckner.)

individuals (Galasko *et al.*, 1990; Morris *et al.*, 1991; Devanand *et al.*, 1997; Herlitz *et al.*, 1997). This has, in part, prompted the consideration that aging and AD are part of the same spectrum (Ebly *et al.*, 1994), with cognitive decline and 'senility' suggested to be an inevitable result of the aging process. In fact, when strict criteria are employed to exclude even minimally demented individuals from longitudinal studies of cognitively normal elderly, psychometric performance is shown to be surprisingly stable (Howieson *et al.*, 1997; Rubin *et al.*, 1998; Storandt *et al.*, 2002). Thus, substantial cognitive decline need not be a part of truly healthy brain aging (Crystal *et al.*, 1988; Morris *et al.*, 1993; Howieson *et al.*, 1997; Rubin *et al.*, 1998; Haan *et al.*, 1999), suggesting that AD is not inevitable with age.

Clinical studies support a distinction between aging and AD. Cognitively healthy elderly individuals maintain generally stable cognitive performance when followed longitudinally over time (**1.7**). At dementia onset, however, a steep decline in cognitive performance occurs, suggesting the onset of disease is distinct from the aging process (**1.8**). While subtle changes can be expected with age, cognitive decline interfering even mildly with the ability to perform daily functions appears to be a marker of disease.

Alzheimer's disease and mild cognitive impairment

AD represents the most common cause of dementia, accounting for 55–70% of cases of dementia. AD is often accompanied by other age-related disorders. Vascular lesions and Parkinson's disease most commonly coexist with AD, each occurring in about 25% of AD cases. 'Pure' AD accounts for about 50–60% of clinically diagnosed cases of dementia. These concomitant disorders contribute to the expression of AD, as the histopathologic burden of AD lesions for a given level of dementia severity is lower when AD is mixed with other disorders (Nagy *et al.*, 1997; Snowdon *et al.*, 1997; Berg *et al.*, 1998). Given heterogeneity of clinical features and common pathologic overlap, the true occurrence of the non-AD dementias is difficult to ascertain. Dementia with Lewy bodies, vascular dementia, and the frontotemporal dementias are considered to be the most common forms of non-AD dementias (*Tables 1.2, 1.3*).

The term mild cognitive impairment (MCI) is one of many introduced to characterize the boundary of aging and dementia (Kral, 1962; Crook & Bartus, 1986; Flicker *et al.*, 1991; Levy, 1994; Graham *et al.*, 1997; Petersen *et al.*, 1999, 2001a). MCI was specifically intended to capture those patients destined to develop dementia (Flicker *et al.*, 1991). The onset of symptomatic AD is insidious and patients with AD almost always progress through a period of subtle cognitive impairments that do not interfere importantly with their daily functioning. Thus, the concept of MCI includes individuals in this prodromal stage that occurs prior to the diagnosis of overt dementia. Broadly defined, MCI includes (1) evidence of cognitive impairment; (2) preservation of general cognition and functional abilities; and (3) absence of diagnosed dementia. Prevalence estimates for MCI demonstrate considerable variability, ranging from 2.8% to as high as 23.4% (Ebly *et al.*, 1995; Ritchie *et al.*, 2001; Unverzagt *et al.*, 2001; Larrieu *et al.*, 2002; Lopez *et al.*, 2003). Estimates of the risk of 'conversion' from MCI to AD are also widely variable, ranging from 3.7% per year (Ritchie *et al.*, 2001) to 25% in selected samples (Flicker *et al.*, 1991; Dawe *et al.*, 1992). The wide variability in MCI prevalence and estimates of the risk for developing overt AD is due to differences in MCI definitions, study design (retrospective vs. prospective), and the sample studied (referral-based vs. population-based) (Luis *et al.*, 2003).

While MCI captures individuals with the earliest changes of AD or other forms of dementia (i.e. vascular dementia, frontotemporal dementia, dementia with Lewy bodies), it encompasses many different conditions including static cognitive impairment, the 'worried well', and reversible forms of cognitive dysfunction such as those related to depression or medical illnesses. In general, however, it seems clear that individuals with MCI progress to overt AD at a rate far above the baseline dementia incidence rate. Although the concept of MCI is not without controversy, it has served to focus attention on the delineation of the earliest symptoms of AD from the change of normal cognitive aging.

Table 1.2 Differential diagnosis of cognitive decline

- Neurodegenerative dementia (see *Table 1.3*)
- Cerebrovascular disorders:
  - Vascular dementia
  - Binswanger's disease
- Infectious disorders:
  - Chronic meningitis
  - Encephalitis:
      Human immunodeficiency virus
      Lyme disease
  - Progressive multifocal leukoencephalopathy
  - Neurosyphilis
  - Whipple's disease
- Toxic/metabolic encephalopathies
  - Drugs/medications
  - Endocrine: thyroid, parathyroid:
      Nutritional: B_{12} and thiamine deficiencies
      Fluid and electrolyte abnormalities
      Hypoglycemia
      Other: carbon monoxide, heavy metals (lead, mercury, arsenic, thallium)
- Inflammatory:
  - Vasculitis:
      Primary central nervous system vasculitis
      Systemic vasculitides:
        Systemic lupus erythematosus
        Polyarteritis nodosa
        Wegener's granulomatosus
        Churg–Strauss syndrome
        Sarcoidosis

- Demyelinating:
  - Multiple sclerosis
- Neoplastic:
  - Direct effects of primary and metastatic disease
  - Paraneoplastic syndromes
- Hydrocephalus
- Affective disorders (depression)
- Neurogenetic disorders:
  - Spinocerebellar ataxias
  - Dentatorubral-pallidoluysian atrophy
  - Hallervorden–Spatz disease
  - Gangliosidoses
  - Adult neuronal ceroid lipofuscinosis (Kuf's disease)
  - Mitochondrial encephalopathies
  - Porphyrias
  - Wilson's disease

Table 1.3 Neurodegenerative dementias

- Alzheimer's disease
- Dementia with Lewy bodies
- Vascular dementia
- Frontotemporal lobar degeneration:
  - Frontotemporal dementia
  - Semantic dementia
  - Progressive nonfluent aphasia
- Progressive supranuclear palsy

- Corticobasal degeneration
- Parkinson's disease with dementia
- Multiple system atrophy
- Huntington's disease
- Prion disorders:
  - Creutzfeldt–Jakob disease
  - Fatal familial insomnia
  - Gerstmann–Sträussler–Scheinker disease

Diagnosis and evaluation of dementing disorders

The key information for diagnosing dementia comes primarily from the clinical information, resting largely on determining whether cognitive decline is present to such a degree as to interfere with function in usual activities. The 2001 American Academy of Neurology (AAN) practice parameter on the diagnosis of dementia recommended the routine use of the DSM criteria (Knopman *et al.*, 2001b). The criteria's key principles include (1) cognitive decline; and (2) interference with functioning as the ultimate validation of the presence of dementia (*Table 1.4*). Assessing whether these criteria are met involves (1) evaluating the presenting problem; (2) obtaining information from someone who knows the patient well (i.e. obtaining an informant-based history); (3) physical and neurologic examinations; and (4) evaluation of the cognitive, behavioral, and functional status of the patient. Dementia remains a clinical diagnosis and no test replaces an assessment by an experienced physician.

Table 1.4 Clinical hallmarks of dementia

- Gradual onset
- Progressive decline
- Memory loss
- Other cognitive domains impaired
- Interferes with function

Table 1.5 Features suggestive of other dementing illness

- Parkinsonism → dementia with Lewy bodies, corticobasal degeneration
- Language:
  Naming impairment → progressive nonfluent aphasia
  Comprehension impairment → semantic dementia
- Apraxia → corticobasal degeneration
- Myoclonus → prion disease (Creutzfeldt–Jakob disease)

Importance of an informant-based history

Establishing a history of a significant cognitive decline must be individualized because each individual's usual activities vary according to native intelligence and their educational and occupational experiences. It is therefore important to gather information about cognitive changes from someone who knows the patient well, such as the spouse or a family member. The memory loss of early-stage AD is generally well compensated. Individuals may continue to perform independently in the community and symptoms may not be readily apparent in casual contact with others. Discussing cognitive changes with an attentive family member, relative, or friend is essential in making a confident diagnosis using their descriptions of cognitive changes to establish whether cognitive changes are interfering even mildly with the patient's usual function. The perceptions of a knowledgeable informant are sensitive and reliable for detecting early dementia (McGlone *et al.*, 1990; Koss *et al.*, 1993; Tierney *et al.*, 1996; Jorm, 1997; Carr *et al.*, 2000). Additionally, self-reported memory complaints do not correlate well with actual cognitive performance and are not a strong predictor of the development of dementia (Bolla *et al.*, 1991; Flicker *et al.*, 1993). On the other hand, these self-reported complaints should not necessarily be dismissed as benign as patients with early AD often retain some insight into their cognitive difficulties.

Neurologic examination

In mild and even moderate AD, focal neurologic abnormalities are infrequent and the neurologic examination is performed primarily to evaluate for any signs suggestive of another dementing illness (*Table 1.5*). The neurologic examination should therefore be focused on evaluating for the presence of focal upper motor neuron signs, extrapyramidal signs, and prominent aphasia and apraxia.

Mild impairments in language and praxis are commonly encountered in AD, although memory loss remains the prominent symptom. Language impairments often begin with mild word-finding difficulties, manifested as circumlocutions (substituting the desired word with a description or series of shorter words) and halting speech. Unexplained language impairments with relative sparing of memory may indicate the presence of a variant of frontotemporal lobar degeneration such as nonfluent progressive aphasia or semantic dementia.

Apraxia, a disorder of skilled movement despite intact strength, sensation, and coordination, will develop as typical AD progresses but is not a prominent early manifestation. Apraxia in mild AD patients is commonly characterized as substitution of the individual's hand as object, for instance using their fist to represent a hammer rather than grasping an imaginary hammer. Severe apraxia, often unilateral, may indicate corticobasal degeneration.

Focal neurologic deficits such as mild hemiparesis, unilateral visual field deficit, or Babinski sign may indicate the presence of significant vascular disease which commonly coexists with AD, and may play a role in the symptomatic expression of AD (Snowdon et al., 1997). The presence of increased tone and a Parkinsonian gait early in the course may indicate dementia with Lewy bodies or Parkinson's dementia. Extrapyramidal signs are common in advanced AD but are generally not prominent early in the course; prominent unilateral extrapyramidal signs may indicate corticobasal degeneration. Prominent myoclonus may indicate Creutzfeldt–Jakob disease, especially if accompanying a rapidly progressive dementing illness, although myoclonus can also be encountered in the late stages of AD.

Laboratory and radiological evaluation

Structural neuroimaging is recommended in the form of either MRI or noncontrast computed tomography (CT). The basis of this recommendation is the evidence that up to 5% of patients with dementia have a clinically significant structural lesion that would not have been predicted based on the history or examination (Chui & Zhang, 1997). These potential lesions include brain neoplasms, subdural hematomas, or normal pressure hydrocephalus. However, fully reversible dementia due to unsuspected causes is rare. The AAN practice paramenter reported insufficient evidence to recommend single photon emission computed tomography (SPECT) or positron emission tomography (PET) in the routine evaluation of dementia patients. Additionally, PET and SPECT imaging have not been shown to be cost-effective for dementia diagnosis (McMahon et al., 2000).

Depression, B_{12} deficiency, and hypothyroidism are common co-morbidities in patients with suspected

---

Table 1.6 Basic laboratory assessment for cognitive impairment

- Neuroimaging:
  - CT or MRI
- Laboratory:
  - Thyroid
  - Vitamin B_{12}
  - Syphilis (only if clinically indicated)

---

dementia, and screening for these treatable disorders is recommended (Table 1.6) (Knopman et al., 2001). Depression coexists with AD in up to 12% of demented patients (Forsell and Winblad, 1998), and a few reports have attributed dementia to B_{12} deficiency and hypothyroidism (Clarfield, 1988). In most individuals, treatment of these disorders is unlikely to reverse cognitive deficits completely, and cognitive improvement in demented patients with B_{12} and thyroid replacement are equivocal (Knopman et al., 2001a). Nevertheless, the high frequency of these co-morbidities and the potential for amelioration of cognitive symptoms necessitates screening. Routine screening for syphilis is no longer recommended, a change from the 1994 practice parameter (American Academy of Neurology/Quality Standards Subcommittee, 1994) unless syphilis risk factors or evidence of infection exists.

Psychometric/mental status testing

Mental status tests should be used primarily to confirm the presence of cognitive deficits and not as a method of diagnosis. Mental status tests cannot, certainly at the initial evaluation, indicate whether the individual has declined from previous levels of cognitive abilities nor determine the presence of impairment sufficient to interfere with accustomed activities. This information must be collected from the informant interview. Testing is useful in demonstrating a pattern of deficits consistent with an AD pattern (primary deficits in memory and executive function) and to monitor dementia progression over time through serial testing. Over-reliance on cognitive test performance in addition to failure to incorporate an informant's observations about an individual's cognitive function in relation to past abilities results in the under-recognition of mild AD.

The determination of normal and abnormal performance on psychometric tests uses arbitrary cutoff points and standard deviations for a group means of memory performance. These means are not always applicable to an individual. Cognitive tests, such as the Mini-mental State Examination (MMSE) (Folstein *et al.*, 1975) are influenced by age, education (Doraiswamy *et al.*, 1995), race (Manly *et al.*, 1998), and gender, and show large measurement error (*Table 1.7*). These factors often make cognitive tests insensitive to early-stage AD (Galasko *et al.*, 1990; Devanand *et al.*, 1997; Herlitz *et al.*, 1997). The performance of nondemented aging and very mild and mild AD individuals on widely used cognitive scales such as the MMSE and the Blessed Scale-cognitive portion (Blessed *et al.*, 1968) show considerable overlap between the groups. This suggests that over-reliance on neuropsychologic tests would exclude some individuals experiencing interference with their usual functions who are still performing within the arbitrary range of normal.

Summary

The key information for diagnosing dementia comes primarily from the clinical assessment. In establishing a diagnosis, clinicians should obtain a history from someone who knows the patient well as the perceptions of a knowledgeable informant are sensitive and reliable for detecting early dementia (McGlone *et al.*, 1990; Koss *et al.*, 1993; Tierney *et al.*, 1996; Jorm,1997; Carr *et al.*, 2000). While brain aging is associated with structural and functional changes, cognitive changes seen normally with age are generally mild and should not be expected to interfere, even mildly, with an individual's accustomed activities of daily living.

There is currently a great interest in the potential utility of biomarkers, neuroimaging, and genetics in augmenting, or even replacing, the clinical diagnosis of dementing disorders. Clinical methods, however, remain the gold standard for the antemortem diagnosis of dementia and AD. Additionally, clinical and pathologic classifications will remain the backbone of interpreting these methods and in advancing our understanding of the complex interplay between genotype and phenotype.

Table 1.7 Selective cognitive instruments used in detection of dementia

Instrument (cutoff)	Sensitivity (%)	Specificity (%)
MMSE (<24) (Kukull *et al.*, 1994)	63	96
MMSE (bottom 10%) (Ganguli *et al.*, 1993)	49	92
MMSE (decline of 4 points)/1–4 years (Tangalos *et al.*, 1996)	82	99
Seven-minute screen (Solomon *et al.*, 1998)	92	96
Clock drawing test (Shulman, 2000)	85	85
CDR (Juva *et al.*, 1995)	92	94
IQCODE (Fuh *et al.*, 1995)	89	88

CDR: Clinical Dementia Rating Scale; IQCODE: Informant Questionnaire on Cognitive Decline in the Elderly.
(From Petersen *et al.*, 2001b)

References

American Academy of Neurology/Quality Standards Subcommittee (1994). Practice parameter for diagnosis and evaluation of dementia. *Neurology* **44**:2203–2206.

American Psychiatric Association (1994). *Diagnostic and Statistical Manual of Mental Disorders.* Washington, DC: American Psychiatric Association.

Bartzokis G, Beckson M, Lu PH, *et al.* (2001). Age-related changes in frontal and temporal lobe volumes in men: a magnetic resonance imaging study. *Arch. Gen. Psychiatry* **58**:461–465.

Bartzokis G, Cummings JL, Sultzer D, *et al.* (2003). White matter structural integrity in healthy aging adults and patients with Alzheimer disease: a magnetic resonance imaging study. *Arch. Neurol.* **60**:393–398.

Berg L, McKeel DW Jr., Miller JP, *et al.* (1998). Clinicopathologic studies in cognitively healthy aging and Alzheimer disease: relation of histological markers to dementia severity, age, sex, and apolipoprotein E genotype. *Arch. Neurol.* **55**:326–335.

Bick KL, Amaducci L (1989). *The Early Story of Alzheimer's Disease.* Liviana Press, Padova.

Blessed G, Tomlinson BE, Roth M (1968). The association between quantitative measures of dementia and of senile change in the cerebral grey matter of the elderly subjects. *Br. J. Psychiatry* **114**:797–811.

Bolla KI, Lindgren KN, Bonaccorsy C, *et al.* (1991). Memory complaints in older adults: fact or fiction? *Arch. Neurol.* **48**:61–64.

Burns JM, Church JA, Johnson DK, *et al.* (2005). White matter lesions are prevalent but differentially related with cognition in aging and early Alzheimer disease. *Arch Neurol* **62**(12):1870–1876.

Carr DB, Gray S, Baty J, *et al.* (2000). The value of informant vs. individual's complaints of memory impairment in early dementia. *Neurology* **55**:1724–1726.

Chui H, Zhang Q (1997). Evaluation of dementia: a systematic study of the usefulness of the American Academy of Neurology's practice parameters. *Neurology* **49**:925–935.

Clarfield AM (1988). The reversible dementias: do they reverse? *Ann. Intern. Med.* **109**:476–486.

Crook TH, Bartus RT (1986). Age-associated memory impairment: proposed diagnostic criteria and measures of clinical change; Report of a National Institute of Mental Health work group. *Dev. Neuropsychol.* **2**:261–276.

Crystal H, Dickson D, Fuld P, *et al.* (1988). Clinico-pathologic studies in dementia: nondemented subjects with pathologically confirmed Alzheimer's disease. *Neurology* **38**:1682–1687.

Dawe B, Procter A, Philpot M (1992). Concepts of mild memory impairment in the elderly and their relationship to dementia: a review. *Int. J. Geriatr. Psychiatry* **7**:473–479.

Devanand DP, Folz M, Gorlyn M, *et al.* (1997). Questionable dementia: clinical course and predictors of outcome. *J. Am. Geriatr. Soc.* **45**:321–328.

Doraiswamy PM, Krishen A, Stallone F, *et al.* (1995). Cognitive performance on the Alzheimer's disease assessment scale: effect of education. *Neurology* **45**:1980–1984.

Ebly EM, Hogan DB, Parhad IM (1995). Cognitive impairment in the nondemented elderly. Results from the Canadian Study of Health and Aging. *Arch. Neurol.* **52**:612–619.

Ebly EM, Parhad IM, Hogan DB, *et al.* (1994). Prevalence and types of dementia in the very old. Results from the Canadian Study of Health and Aging. *Neurology* **44**:1593–1600.

Esiri MM, Nagy Z, Smith MZ, *et al.* (1999). Cerebrovascular disease and threshold for dementia in the early stages of Alzheimer's disease. *Lancet* **354**:919–920.

Evans DA, Funkenstein HH, Albert MS, *et al.* (1989). Prevalence of Alzheimer's disease in a community population of older persons: higher than previously reported. *JAMA* **262**:2551–2556.

Flicker C, Ferris SH, Reisberg B (1991). Mild cognitive impairment in the elderly: predictors of dementia. *Neurology* **41**:1006–1009.

Flicker C, Ferris SH, Reisberg B (1993). A longitudinal study of cognitive function in elderly persons with subjective memory complaints. *J. Am. Geriatr. Soc.* **41**:1029–1032.

Folstein MF, Folstein SE, McHugh PR (1975). Mini-mental state: a practical method for grading the cognitive state of patients for the clinicians. *J. Psychiatr. Res.* **12**:189–198.

Forsell Y, Winblad B (1998). Major depression in a population of demented and nondemented older people: prevalence and correlates. *J. Am. Geriatr. Soc.* **46**:27–30.

Fotenos AF, Snyder AZ, Girton LE, *et al.* (2005). Normative estimates of cross-sectional and longitudinal brain volume decline in aging and AD. *Neurology* **64**:1032–1039.

Fuh JL, Teng EL, Lin KN, *et al.* (1995). The Informant Questionnaire on Cognitive Decline in the Elderly (IQCODE) as a screening tool for dementia for a predominantly illiterate Chinese population. *Neurology* **45**:92–96.

Galasko D, Klauber MR, Hofstetter R (1990). The Mini-mental state examination in the early diagnosis of Alzheimer's disease. *Arch. Neurol.* **47**:49–52.

Ganguli M, Belle S, Ratcliff G, *et al.* (1993). Sensitivity and specificity for dementia of population-based criteria for cognitive impairment: the MoVIES project. *J. Gerontol.* **48**:M152–M161.

Graham JE, Rockwood K, Beattie LB, *et al.* (1997). Prevalence and severity of cognitive impairment with and without dementia in an elderly population. *Lancet* **349**:1793–1796.

Haan MN, Shemanki L, Jagust WJ, *et al.* (1999). The role of APOE e4 in modulating effects of other risk factors for cognitive decline in elderly persons. *JAMA* **282**:40–46.

Hebert LE, Beckett LA, Scherr PA, *et al.* (2001). Annual incidence of Alzheimer disease in the United States projected to the years 2000 through 2050. *Alz. Dis. Assoc. Disord.* **15**:169–173.

Herlitz A, Small BJ, Fratiglioni L, *et al.* (1997). Detection of mild dementia in community surveys. *Arch. Neurol.* **54**:319–324.

Hildebrand C, Remahl S, Persson H, *et al.* (1993). Myelinated nerve fibres in the CNS. *Prog. Neurobiol.* **40**:319–384.

Howieson DB, Dame A, Camicioli R, *et al.* (1997). Cognitive markers preceding Alzheimer's dementia in the healthy oldest old. *J. Am. Geriatr. Soc.* **45**:584–589.

Jernigan TL, Archibald SL, Fennema-Notestine C, *et al.* (2001). Effects of age on tissues and regions of the cerebrum and cerebellum. *Neurobiology of Aging* **22**:581–594.

Jorm AF (1997). Methods of screening for dementia: a meta-analysis of studies comparing an informant questionnaire with a brief cognitive test. *Alz. Dis. Assoc. Disord.* **11**:158–162.

Juva K, Sulkava R, Erkinjuntti T, *et al.* (1995). Usefulness of the Clinical Dementia Rating scale in screening for dementia. *Int. Psychogeriatr.* **7**:17–24.

Knopman DS, DeKosky ST, Cummings JL, *et al.* (2001). Practice parameter: diagnosis of dementia (an evidence-based review). Report of the Quality Standards Subcommittee of the American Academy of Neurology. *Neurology* **56**:1143–1153.

Koss E, Patterson MB, Ownby R, *et al.* (1993). Memory evaluation in Alzheimer's disease: caregivers' appraisals and objective testing. *Arch. Neurol.* **50**:92–97.

Kral VA (1962). Senescent forgetfulness: benign and malignant. *Can. Med. Assoc. J.* **86**:257–260.

Kukull WA, Larson EB, Teri L, *et al.* (1994). The mini-mental state examination score and the clinical diagnosis of dementia. *J. Clin. Epidemiol.* **47**:1061–1067.

Larrieu S, Letenneur L, Orgogozo JM, *et al.* (2002). Incidence and outcome of mild cognitive impairment in a population-based prospective cohort. *Neurology* **59**:1594-1599.

Levy R (1994). Aging-associated cognitive decline. *Int. Psychogeriatr.* **6**:63-68.

Longstreth WT, Manolio TA, Arnold A, *et al.* (1996). Clinical correlates of white matter findings on cranial magnetic resonance imaging of 3301 elderly people: The Cardiovascular Health Study. *Stroke* **27**:1274–1282.

Lopez OL, Jagust WJ, Dulberg C, *et al.* (2003). Risk factors for mild cognitive impairment in the Cardiovascular Health Study Cognition Study: Part 2. *Arch. Neurol.* **60**:1394–1399.

Luis CA, Loewenstein DA, Acevedo A, *et al.* (2003). Mild cognitive impairment: directions for future research. *Neurology* **61**:438–444.

Manly JJ, Jacobs DM, Sano M, *et al.* (1998). Cognitive test performance among nondemented elderly African Americans and whites. *Neurology* **50**:1238–1245.

McGlone J, Gupta S, Humphrey D, *et al.* (1990). Screening for early dementia using memory complaints from patients and relatives. *Arch. Neurol.* **47**:1189–1193.

McMahon PM, Araki SS, Neumann PJ, *et al.* (2000). Cost-effectiveness of functional imaging tests in the diagnosis of Alzheimer disease. *Radiology* **217**:58–68.

Morris JC (2000). Nosology of dementia. In: *Neurologic Clinics*. ST DeKosky (ed). W.B. Saunders Company, Philadelphia, pp. 773–788.

Morris JC, Edland S, Clark C, *et al.* (1993). The Consortium to Establish a Registry for Alzheimer's Disease (CERAD). Part IV. Rates of cognitive change in the longitudinal assessment of probable Alzheimer's disease. *Neurology* **43**:2457–2465.

Morris JC, McKeel DW Jr., Storandt M, *et al.* (1991). Very mild Alzheimer's disease: informant-based clinical, psychometric, and pathological distinction from normal aging. *Neurology* **41**:469-478.

Nagy Z, Esiri MM, Jobst KA, *et al.* (1997). The effects of additional pathology on the cognitive deficit in Alzheimer disease. *J. Neuropathol. Exp. Neurol.* **56**:165–170.

Park DC, Plk TA, Mikels, *et al.* (2001). Cerebral aging: brain and behavioral models of cognitive function. *Dialog. Clin. Neurosci.* **3**:151–165.

Petersen RC, Smith GE, Waring SC *et al.* (1999). Mild cognitive impairment – clinical characterization and outcome. *Arch. Neurol.* **56**(3):303–3-8.

Petersen RC, Doody R, Kurz A, *et al.* (2001a) Current concepts in mild cognitive impairment. *Arch. Neurol.* **58**(12):1985–1992.

Petersen RC, Stevens JC, Ganguli M, *et al.* (2001b). Practice parameter: Early detection of dementia: mild cognitive impairment (an evidence-based review). Report of the Quality Standards Subcommittee of the American Academy of Neurology. *Neurology* **56**:1133–1142.

Prigerson HG (2003). Costs to society of family caregiving for patients with end-stage Alzheimer's disease. *N. Engl. J. Med.* **349**:1891–1892.

Ritchie K, Artero S, Touchon J (2001). Classification criteria for mild cognitive impairment. A population-based validation study. *Neurology* **56**:37–42.

Rubin EH, Storandt M, Miller JP, *et al.* (1993). Influence of age on clinical and psychometric assessment of subjects with very mild or mild dementia of the Alzheimer type. *Arch. Neurol.* **50**:380–383.

Rubin EH, Storandt M, Miller JP, *et al.* (1998). A prospective study of cognitive function and onset of dementia in cognitively healthy elders. *Arch. Neurol.* **55**:395–401.

Shulman K (2000). Clock-drawing: is it the ideal cognitive screening test? *Int. J. Geriatr. Psychiatry* **15**:548–561.

Snowdon DA, Greiner LH, Mortimer JA, *et al.* (1997). Brain infarction and the clinical expression of Alzheimer disease. *JAMA* **277**:813–817.

Solomon PR, Hirschoff A, Kelly B, *et al.* (1998) A 7 minute neurocognitive screening battery highly sensitive to Alzheimer's disease. *Arch. Neurol.* **55**:349–355.

Storandt M, Grant EA, Miller JP, *et al.* (2002). Rates of progression in mild cognitive impairment and early Alzheimer's disease. *Neurology* **59**:1034–1041.

Tangalos EG, Smith GE, Ivnik RJ, *et al.* (1996) The Mini-Mental State Examination in general medical practice: clinical utility and acceptance. *Mayo Clin. Proc.* **71**:829–837.

Tierney MC, Szalai JP, Snow WG, *et al.* (1996). The prediction of Alzheimer disease. *Arch. Neurol.* **53**:423–427.

Unverzagt FW, Gao S, Baiyewu O, *et al.* (2001). Prevalence of cognitive impairment: data from the Indianapolis Study of Health and Aging. *Neurology* **57**:1655–1662.

Vermeer SE, Koudstaal PJ, Oudkerk M, *et al.* (2002). Prevalence and risk factors of silent brain infarcts in the population-based Rotterdam Scan Study. *Stroke* **33**:21–25.

Zekry D, Duyckaerts C, Moulias R, *et al.* (2002). Degenerative and vascular lesions of the brain have synergistic effects in dementia of the elderly. *Acta Neuropathol. (Berl.)* **103**:481–487.

Chapter 2

Interviewing, screening, and staging of dementia: a focus on Alzheimer's disease

Introduction

'That January, my fifty-seventh birthday, was pleasant and eventful and I began to adjust to middle age ... I was active and happy ... Then came a beautiful spring day later that year. It was the day after the tests were finished and the results reviewed. It was the day that I was diagnosed with Alzheimer's. What time had now hidden was now revealed. Genetic secrets, locked inside before my birth, were now in the open. I became a new member in a parade of horror created by Alzheimer's' (DeBaggio, 2002, p. 1).

So begins a moving account of early-onset Alzheimer's disease (AD) by Thomas DeBaggio, a commercial herb grower and author from Virginia, US. For DeBaggio and millions like him in the US and across the globe, the advent of AD is a harsh reality. Minor problems with recent memory at first give way, over time, to generalized cognitive and functional decline, ending years later in profound loss of individual and interpersonal identity. Although affected individuals, like DeBaggio, may retain reasonable awareness of the disease and its impact early on, within months to a few years such awareness wanes, and the extended family is left to march in the 'parade of horror' alone. The affected individual is present in body, a subject of notice and care, but cognitively separate from the day-to-day realities of constant supervision, visits to the doctor, alterations in daily routine to accommodate new deficits, placement in a long-term care facility, and so on. AD is a disease of the individual *and* the family.

The early signs and symptoms of clinical AD are subtle and often difficult to distinguish from changes expected in normal aging, disturbances of mood, and/or quirks of personality. Close family members are typically the first to notice one or more warning signs (*Table 2.1*), but may not act to obtain a diagnosis until a number of these signs are evident and appreciated. Also, individuals with early AD will tend to compensate for deficits (e.g. by writing down information to be remembered, making more extensive use of a calendar), as well as downplaying or otherwise explaining away problems observed by others. Such efforts may further delay initiation of an evaluation process. In addition, local relatives may perceive a problem much earlier than those living at a distance. Disagreements can arise in a family network about what is going on and if medical intervention is truly needed. Despite such factors, the impetus for an older adult to be evaluated medically for memory loss and dementia typically rests with the family. When a family member raises a concern, the clinician providing care would do well to pay attention.

Once an evaluation is arranged and positive results known, family caregivers are forced, ready or not, to confront the harsh realities of AD: a prospect of progressive decline and a likelihood of increasing demands for care and support over time. The experience of family caregivers has been labeled 'the long goodbye' in a number of publications, most recently by President Ronald Reagan's daughter, Patti Davis (Davis, 2004). One of the most challenging aspects for family members is an ever-present and progressive loss of relationship with the affected individual. Vibrant, engaged loved ones gradually change into distant, superficial shells of their former selves. Close relatives, spouses, and adult children especially, have been shown to experience significant grief reactions in response to such losses (Meuser & Marwit, 2001; Marwit & Meuser, 2002). Providing care to a person with dementia is a stressful, burdensome

Table 2.1 Ten warning signs of AD

- *Memory loss:* one of the most common early signs of dementia is forgetting recently learned information. While it is normal to forget appointments, names, or telephone numbers, those with dementia will forget such things more often and not remember them later.
- *Difficulty performing familiar tasks:* people with dementia often find it hard to complete everyday tasks that are so familiar we usually do not think about how to do them. A person with AD may not know the steps for preparing a meal, using a household appliance, or participating in a lifelong hobby.
- *Problems with language:* everyone has trouble finding the right word sometimes, but a person with AD often forgets simple words or uses word substitutes, making his or her speech or writing hard to understand. If a person with AD is unable to find his or her toothbrush, for example, the individual may ask for 'that thing for my mouth'.
- *Disorientation to time and place:* it is normal to forget the day of the week or where you're going. People with AD can become lost on their own street. They may forget where they are and how they got there, and may not know how to get back home.
- *Poor or decreased judgement:* no one has perfect judgment all of the time. Those with AD may dress without regard to the weather, wearing several shirts on a warm day or very little clothing in cold weather. Those with dementia often show poor judgment about money, giving away large sums to telemarketers or paying for home repairs or products they don't need.

- *Problems with abstract thinking:* balancing a checkbook is a task that can be challenging for some. A person with AD may forget what the numbers represent and what needs to be done with them.
- *Misplacing things:* anyone can temporarily misplace a wallet or key. A person with AD may put things in unusual places, like an iron in the freezer or a wristwatch in the sugar bowl.
- *Changes in mood or behavior:* everyone can become sad or moody from time to time. Someone with AD can show rapid mood swings, from calm to tears to anger, for no apparent reason.
- *Changes in personality:* personalities ordinarily change somewhat with age. A person with AD can change dramatically, becoming extremely confused, suspicious, fearful, or dependent on a family member.
- *Loss of initiative:* it is normal to tire of housework, business activities, or social obligations at times. The person with AD may become very passive, sitting in front of the television for hours, sleeping more than usual, or not wanting to do usual activities.

(Adapted from Alzheimer's Association, 2004. Available on-line at http://www.alz.org/AboutAD/Warning.asp)

experience all around. Grief may be most acute and troublesome for adult children at the moderate stage when in-home care demands are high and huge personal adjustments are required, whereas spouse caregivers appear to experience a peak in grief following long-term care placement, often viewed as symbolic of failure ('I wasn't a good enough caregiver to keep my loved one at home') or of death itself ('My marriage is essentially over … now where am I?'). In addition to grief and burden, caregivers also face an increased risk of physical health problems, disturbed sleep, anxiety, and depression (Connell *et al.*, 2001).

Role of the clinician

Physicians and other providers of medical care to older adults will, at one time or another, be involved in the recognition of key dementia symptoms, assessment towards a diagnosis, initiation and management of treatment, and provision of supportive, behavioral, and psychosocial care to patients and family members alike. The provision of such comprehensive services is not a simple matter and additional training is often helpful. Continuing education providers are increasingly offering dementia-specific educational opportunities (Meuser *et al.*, 2004). Community organizations (e.g. Alzheimer's Association: http://www.alz.org) and government-funded agencies (e.g. Area Agencies on Aging: http://www.n4a.org) are available to help by providing educational information, supportive services including support groups and respite programs, and referral assistance to patients and families.

In order to make a diagnosis of clinical AD, the clinician must show that significant impairment exists in memory functioning and in at least one other cognitive domain (e.g. language, orientation, executive functioning, visual-spatial skills). In addition, such deficits must be associated with decrements in daily life functioning (DSM-IV Criteria, American Psychiatric Association, 1994). In other words, to qualify for a diagnosis of AD, the patient must demonstrate both objective and subjective impairment, with deficits apparent on cognitive testing (and/or from history) and through observations of a family member or close associate.

The detection of cognitive functional deficits in dementia is not difficult *per se*, but does require an investment of time and a willingness to go beyond the typical brief office examination. Extra information is needed, both from the identified patient and an informant, typically a spouse, child, or other close family member. In the sections below, the evaluative and diagnostic approach, application of screening measures, staging of impairment level, and clinical dementia care as a function of patient and family needs are discussed.

Diagnosis of inclusion

It used to be the case that AD was considered a *diagnosis of exclusion* (Keefover, 1990). The clinician would test for, and otherwise rule out, alternative causes for observed symptoms. Tests of thyroid function, vitamin B_{12} level, hypertension, stroke, tumor, and so on, would be pursued first. If, after extensive testing, a metabolic or other acute cause could not be identified, it was assumed by process of elimination that AD was the likely cause of observed cognitive functional decline. The ultimate confirmation, however, would need to wait until histologic examination of brain tissue after death. A number of long-standing community brain banks, for example, continue to offer autopsy services to families for diagnostic confirmation and assessment of genetic risk (Murphy & Ravina, 2003).

Over the past 15–20 years, the diagnosis of AD has shifted to become a *diagnosis of inclusion* (Small *et al.*, 1997). Great strides have been made in identifying symptom and progression patterns. Accepted diagnostic criteria are readily available (e.g. Knopman *et al.*, 2001). It is now possible to diagnose uncomplicated or 'pure' cases of dementia of Alzheimer's type (DAT) with a high degree of accuracy, 85–90% in specialty centres (Morris, 2003). DAT accounts for as many as 65–70% of all cases of dementia among adults aged 65 years and older. Differential diagnosis of mixed dementia (i.e. when Alzheimer's disease co-exists with another neurodegenerative disease process) is more complicated, especially for nonspecialists, and accuracy rates are somewhat lower.

It is important to recognize that AD is a condition of aging. The risk of developing AD increases with advancing age, especially after age 70 years. The prevalence of AD under age 50 years, for example, is less than 2%. The typical cause of AD at this young age is familial transmission of a rare causal genetic mutation (Pastor & Goate, 2004). Sporadic AD, which may result from a variety of causal and contributing factors (genetic, environmental), afflicts 5–10% of individuals aged 65–74 years, 15–20% of those aged 75–84 years, and 40–50% of those aged 85 years and over; or a total of 4.5 million in the US today alone (Herbert *et al.*, 2003).

A common challenge for clinicians, primary care providers, and specialists alike, is recognizing the signs and symptoms of AD when a variety of other medical illnesses are present. In addition to increased risk for dementia, older adults are also at greater risk of a host of other health problems, including cardiovascular disease, hypertension, stroke, and so on, that are demanding of clinical attention. The typical 15-minute doctor–patient encounter may provide enough time for identifying and managing common physical health complaints, but not necessarily dementia. Persons with mild clinical AD often present as 'normal' in a brief encounter and are otherwise unlikely to acknowledge cognitive concerns. If the patient or family doesn't raise a concern about cognitive functional change and the clinician doesn't have the time or inclination to ask, care will remain focused primarily on physical health complaints. Under these conditions, dementia symptoms will eventually be recognized, but only later in the clinical progression when many more brain cells are likely to be dead or dying, thus complicating treatment.

The evaluative mindset

Clinicians with an *evaluative mindset* for AD demonstrate (1) awareness that older adults face a tangible and increasing risk for dementia with age; and (2) vigilance for cognitive functional changes atypical in the aging process alone, or in response to clinical depression. Whereas the average 65-year-old is relatively unlikely to have clinical AD or another form of dementing illness, the average 85-year-old, in contrast, faces a 1 in 2 chance. The clinician evaluating a patient in their eighties for the first time needs to consider the real possibility that AD (or another dementia) is present and investigate accordingly.

Part of this investigation is separating out what is normal for age and what is not. As shown in *Table 2.2*, how a patient reports a memory problem can provide clues (with other data) as to what may be going on[1]. Persons experiencing normal age-associated memory impairment may comment about not remembering as well as in the past but, for them, there is no functional loss. In normal aging, an item may be forgotten or unavailable for recall in an immediate sense, but the memory trace remains and is eventually recalled. For example, one may lose the car keys for a short period, but one eventually finds them. In contrast, in dementia, if a

Table 2.2 Memory complaints in normal aging, depression, and dementia

	Normal aging	*Depression*	*Clinical AD/dementia*
Complaint	May report a mild or subtle memory problem	More likely to complain about memory problems – 'I'm having terrible problems with my memory'	Expresses variable, nonspecific memory complaints – 'I forget sometimes' Or, may show little or no awareness of a memory problem –'I'm fine'
Functional interference	The problem does not interfere with daily functioning	Reported problems may interfere with daily functioning, but only minimally. Functional problems are more likely attributable to the mood disorder (lack of motivation, apathy, lethargy)	Clearly interferes with daily functioning (repeating the same questions or comments, missing appointments, forgetting to take medications on time, not paying bills appropriately or double paying them)
Cognitive status	Onset of the problem is unclear. Cognition normal on testing	Onset may be reported as sudden or abrupt. Subtle deficits may be apparent on testing, but these do not fit a typical dementia pattern	Gradual onset and progression. Cognition impaired on testing with gradual decline observed over time
Mood	Not associated with significant depressive or anxiety symptoms	Often associated with depressed or anxious mood	May be associated with fluctuating or blunted affect. Less likely to acknowledge overt depression, but a mood disorder may be present and contributing

(Adapted from Anstey & Low, 2004.)

[1] This paragraph simplifies the distinction between impairment stemming from normal aging, dementia, and depression. A whole book could be written about such distinctions. It is important for clinicians to consider these processes when evaluating a patient and make a best determination, based on available evidence, as to which may be involved. This determination may change over time as more evidence becomes available.

person loses the car keys, they do not recall where they are over time and it is just a chance occurrence if they find them. Persons with dementia typically do not complain of cognitive problems, others do. Family members notice functional changes and, as noted above, may raise the first red flag to the clinician or other health provider. Finally, persons with clinical depression may present as forgetful and even complain quite vehemently about memory loss, but their concerns are less likely to be corroborated by family reports and/or cognitive test results. It is important to note that these factors, aging, dementia, and depression can also co-exist and contribute together to observed impairment.

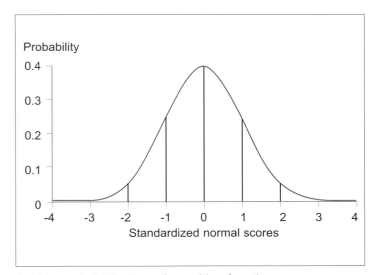

2.1 Normal distribution of cognitive function.

Change from baseline

When clinical AD is suspected, there are a number of ways to make a determination that impairment is truly present. A common strategy used in psychometric/cognitive testing is to compare an individual's observed performance with normative data from other like individuals (i.e. same gender, similar age, same level of education). Most tests of cognitive functioning, when administered to large samples of individuals, yield an inverted U or bell shaped curve (**2.1**). When plotted, many scores cluster around a mean or mid-point, with fewer scores at each end or 'tail' of the distribution. Scores at the high end, two standard deviations above the mean, may represent above average or superior performance, whereas those at the low end, two standard deviations below the mean, may be viewed as below average or indicative of significant impairment.

For the sake of discussion, let us assume that patient A, suspected of having dementia, scores in the below average range (one standard deviation below the mean) on a test for memory of a short story. From a psychometric standpoint, patient A would be viewed as having an objective deficit in memory only if A's score fell two standard deviations below what would be expected based on gender, age, and education norms. If A *should* have performed in the above average range because of high educational attainment (i.e. one standard deviation above the mean), but now scores in the below average range, this would be evidence consistent with a memory deficit and suggestive of a possible dementia process (assuming the support of other evaluative data).

An alternative to the psychometric approach is to characterize changes in cognitive functional status based on an *individual* determination. The early symptoms of clinical

AD can be subtle and may not be evident in psychometric test performance. A person with high educational attainment, for example, can still score in the average range and yet also be starting to dement. A change-from-baseline approach allows the clinician to ask 'Is this individual functioning differently now from how he/she did 5–10 years ago?' and seek answers through history provided by patient and family. For example, let's say that patient B presents with a 1–2 year history of memory changes, but is still living independently and requires only minor assistance from family members to get by. B reports a problem, but denies that it is significant. His psychometric test scores are in the average, unimpaired range. His daughter, in contrast, reports a substantial change in functional status from just a few years ago 'He used to build intricate wooden models in the basement, but stopped because he can no longer remember well enough to execute the many steps involved. He can still do other simple things just fine, but not complex tasks like making models. This is a real change for him.' Such a report, in combination with other evidence, would be suggestive of a dementing process under a change-from-baseline approach. It is this approach, supplemented by psychometric/cognitive test scores when appropriate, that the authors advocate and will discuss for the remainder of this chapter.

In-office screening, interviewing, and staging

'The best diagnostic test is a careful history and physical and mental status examination by a physician with knowledge of and interest in dementia and the dementing diseases. Such an evaluation is time consuming, but nothing can replace it' (NIH Consensus Statement, 1987, p. 3413).

A simple flow chart for in-office assessment is shown in **2.2**. The first step is to determine a need for dementia-related evaluation. Is there evidence from patient or family report of a cognitive functional problem? If so, a focused interview with patient and a family informant would be warranted. What changes have been observed? In what areas of

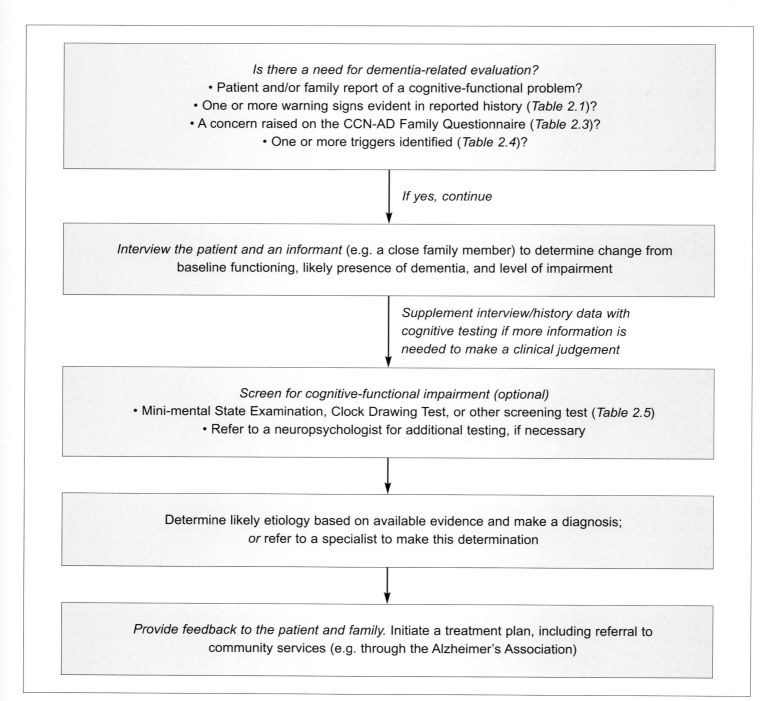

Is there a need for dementia-related evaluation?
• Patient and/or family report of a cognitive-functional problem?
• One or more warning signs evident in reported history (*Table 2.1*)?
• A concern raised on the CCN-AD Family Questionnaire (*Table 2.3*)?
• One or more triggers identified (*Table 2.4*)?

If yes, continue

Interview the patient and an informant (e.g. a close family member) to determine change from baseline functioning, likely presence of dementia, and level of impairment

Supplement interview/history data with cognitive testing if more information is needed to make a clinical judgement

Screen for cognitive-functional impairment (optional)
• Mini-mental State Examination, Clock Drawing Test, or other screening test (*Table 2.5*)
• Refer to a neuropsychologist for additional testing, if necessary

Determine likely etiology based on available evidence and make a diagnosis; *or* refer to a specialist to make this determination

Provide feedback to the patient and family. Initiate a treatment plan, including referral to community services (e.g. through the Alzheimer's Association)

2.2 Flow chart for in-office assessment for dementia.

cognition and/or function? For how long? Are there specific examples? Are the observed problems static or getting progressively worse? The Alzheimer's Association's 10 Warning Signs (*Table 2.1*), the Chronic Care Networks for Alzheimer's Disease (CCN-AD) Family Questionnaire (*Table 2.3*), and the Agency for Health Care Policy and Research's dementia evaluation 'triggers' (*Table 2.4*) can be helpful guides to the clinician in this interviewing process. Any of these tools could also be provided to a family informant as a waiting room questionnaire and then used as a point of reference during the interview process.

If, in the opinion of the clinician, there is reasonable evidence from this initial discussion that a dementing disorder is present, psychometric/cognitive testing may be pursued to gather more information (if necessary), or a more detailed evaluation may be initiated to obtain a diagnosis. *Table 2.5* lists a number of available cognitive screening measures for brief, in-office assessment. The Mini-mental State Examination (MMSE) is the most widely used screening test. Others more specific to AD and other dementias include the Short Blessed Test (SBT) and General Practitioner Assessment of Cognition (GP-COG). Which screening measure a clinician chooses is often a matter of personal preference and experience. With all screening measures, however, it is important not to place too much confidence in a single score. False-positives and negatives are possible. The MMSE, for example, has a maximum score of 30 points, but the normal range can vary from the low 20s and up, depending on characteristics of the individual and testing situation. Low education and minority group membership are two factors that require attention in interpretation of lower scores. A score in the impaired range may not indicate true impairment for individuals from certain groups. Cognitive test scores, such as those derived from the MMSE, can inform and help verify a clinical impression based on interview and history data (i.e. using a change-from-baseline approach), but are never sufficient to determine dementia status alone.

Table 2.3 CCN-AD Family Questionnaire

In your opinion does _____ have problems with any of the following?

1. Repeating or asking the same thing over and over?	Not at all 0	Sometimes 1	Frequently 2	Not applicable
2. Remembering appointments, family occasions, holidays?	Not at all 0	Sometimes 1	Frequently 2	Not applicable
3. Writing checks, paying bills, balancing the checkbook?	Not at all 0	Sometimes 1	Frequently 2	Not applicable
4. Shopping independently (e.g. for clothing, groceries)?	Not at all 0	Sometimes 1	Frequently 2	Not applicable
5. Taking medication according to instructions?	Not at all 0	Sometimes 1	Frequently 2	Not applicable
6. Getting lost while walking or driving in familiar locations?	Not at all 0	Sometimes 1	Frequently 2	Not applicable

Relationship to patient:

Total score:

According to CCN-AD guidelines, a total score of 3 or more should prompt the consideration of a more detailed evaluation. (Adapted from CCN-AD, 2003)

Table 2.4 Triggers for dementia evaluation

Does the person have increasing difficulty with any of the activities listed below?

Problem observed? Yes/No	Cognitive functional area
__Y __N	Learning and retaining new information: Is repetitive; has trouble remembering recent conversations, events, appointments; frequently misplaces objects
__Y __N	Handling complex tasks: Has trouble following a complex train of thought or performing tasks that require many steps such as balancing a checkbook or cooking a meal
__Y __N	Reasoning ability: Is unable to respond with a reasonable plan to problems at work or home, such as knowing what to do if the bathroom is flooded; shows uncharacteristic disregard for rules of social conduct
__Y __N	Spatial ability and orientation: Has trouble driving, organizing objects around the house, finding his or her way around familiar places
__Y __N	Language: Has increasing difficulty with finding the words to express what he or she wants to say and with following conversations
__Y __N	Behavior: Appears more passive and less responsive; is more irritable than usual; is more suspicious than usual; misinterprets visual or auditory stimuli

One or more positive (yes) responses would suggest a need for further evaluation to determine a possible cause or diagnosis.
(Adapted from Costa *et al.*, 1996)

A detailed interview with the patient and a knowledgeable family member is the central process for dementia detection and diagnosis. A thorough medical history (including questions about cognitive functional status, past and present) coupled with an opportunity to corroborate information with an informant is typically required. This can be time consuming. The clinician must decide how much information is reasonable to obtain for a given patient and relative to other practice and reimbursement-related constraints.

At Washington University, the authors rely on the Clinical Dementia Rating (CDR) interview and scoring table to obtain and quantify information from the identified patient and a family informant (Hughes *et al.*, 1982; Morris, 1993). The CDR is a 5-point scale used to characterize six domains of cognitive and functional performance applicable to Alzheimer's disease and related dementias: memory, orientation, judgment and problem solving, community affairs, home and hobbies, and personal care. The necessary information to make each rating is obtained through a semi-structured interview of the patient and a reliable informant.

The CDR table provides descriptive anchors that guide the clinician in making appropriate ratings based on available data and clinical judgment. In addition to ratings for each domain, an overall CDR score may be calculated through the use of an algorithm. This overall score is useful for characterizing and tracking a patient's level of impairment, and may be useful when giving diagnostic feedback to patient and family. CDR scores break down as follows:

0 = normal cognitive functioning (age-related changes only)
0.5 = very mild dementia
1 = mild dementia
2 = moderate dementia
3 = severe dementia

Table 2.5 Screening and staging measures

Measure	Notes
Brief screening tests	
Mini-mental State Examination (MMSE)	19 items measuring orientation, memory, concentration, language, and praxis; requires some test materials; ~10 minutes to administer; the most widely used screening test (Folstein *et al.*, 1975)
Short Blessed Test (SBT)	Six-item weighted version of the Information Memory Concentration Test (Blessed, *et al.*, 1968) ~5 minutes to administer; also correlated with Alzheimer's histopathology (Katzman *et al.*, 1983). A version developed through the Washington University Memory and Aging Project may be downloaded from http://alzheimer.wustl.edu.
General Practitioner Assessment of Cognition (GP-COG)	Includes a six-item screening test similar to the SBT, a clock drawing task, and a five-item informant questionnaire; ~10 minutes to administer (Brodaty *et al.*, 2002)
7 Minute Screen	Four tests (orientation, memory, clock drawing, and verbal fluency); ~7–10 minutes to administer (Solomon & Pendlebury, 1998)
Clinical Staging Instruments (global measures of dementia severity)	
Clinical Dementia Rating (CDR)	Five-point ordinal scale; assesses cognitive and functional abilities by a structured informant interview and patient testing in 6 domains with descriptors for each level of severity (Hughes *et al.*, 1982; Morris, 1993)
Global Deterioration Scale (GDS)	Seven-point ordinal scale; has global descriptors for each severity level; a 35-item Brief Cognitive Rating Scale (BCRS) assists in assignment of the global rating (Reisberg *et al.*, 1982)

(Adapted from Buckles *et al.*, 2000)

Information about the CDR and training options for its use may be accessed on-line at http://alzheimer.wustl.edu/cdr. A number of other diagnostic and staging guides for AD are available through journal articles and on-line. Here is a partial list:

American Academy of Neurology – Practice Parameters – *Diagnosis of Dementia* (Knopman *et al.*, 2001); *Early Detection of Dementia: Mild Cognitve Impairment* (Petersen *et al.*, 2001). Available on-line at http://www.aan.com/publications/practice/ index.cfm

Chronic Care Networks for Alzheimer's Disease – *Tools for Early Identification, Assessment, and Treatment* (http://www.nccconline.org/about/alzheimers.htm)

Alzheimer's Association – On-line Catalog of Assessment Tools and Resources (http://www.alz.org/Resources/TopicIndex/Diagnosis.asp #assessment)

Differential diagnosis

Once it is determined that a dementing disorder is present and at what stage (very mild, mild, and so on), it is important for treatment to identify a likely cause. Clinical AD is the most common dementing illness in older age (i.e. after age 65 years) and should be considered first. In its early stages, clinical AD is primarily a disorder of memory. Long-standing, remote memories remain intact, while recent memory is failing. Persons with early clinical AD forget appointments, misplace items, repeat questions or comments in conversation, and have difficulty managing finances and other complex tasks with high memory demands. As time goes on, problems handling multi-part tasks become apparent, language deficits (both receptive and/or expressive) appear, and disorientation occurs. In time, recent memory failure gives way to more pervasive problems in recall. Even long-standing memories from decades ago become patchy and eventually fade altogether as the disease moves from moderate to severe levels.

Personality change (notably withdrawal) and depressed mood can also occur during progression.

Although some dementia cases will present in this 'classic' pattern, many will not. Another less common neurodegenerative disease may be the cause of observed symptoms. AD neuropathology may also co-exist with one or more other dementing pathologies, each contributing to the clinical picture. Some primary care clinicians may choose to refer to a specialist (i.e. neurologist, psychiatrist, geriatrician) when faced with a complex case. Alternatively, some may choose to make a provisional diagnosis based on available information and seek to confirm this over time. *Table 2.6* presents a simplified listing of symptoms atypical for AD and other diseases to consider in differential diagnosis. For example, AD patients rarely experience vivid visual hallucinations, yet this symptom is quite common in dementia with Lewy bodies.

Table 2.6 Differential diagnosis considerations for unusual features

Symptom/feature	Consideration for differential diagnosis
Abrupt onset	Vascular dementia
Stepwise deterioration	Vascular dementia
Prominent behavioral changes	Frontotemporal dementia
Profound apathy	Frontotemporal dementia
Prominent aphasia	Frontotemporal dementia; vascular dementia
Progressive gait disorder	Vascular dementia; hydrocephalus
Prominent fluctuations in level of consciousness or cognitive abilities	Delirium due to infection, medications, or other causes; dementia with Lewy bodies; seizures
Hallucinations or delusions	Delirium due to infection, medications, or other causes; dementia with Lewy bodies
Extrapyramidal signs or gait disturbance	Parkinsonian syndromes; vascular dementia
Eye-movement abnormalities	Progressive supranuclear palsy; Wernicke's encephalopathy

(Adapted from Kawas, 2003)

Engaging the family and community referral sources

A common 'mistake' in clinical dementia care is choosing not to engage family members in the diagnosis and management process. This may occur in response to a specific patient request ('I don't want my family to know that I have a memory problem'), a concern about breaking confidentiality (e.g. relative to the Health Insurance Portability and Accountability Act [HIPAA] confidentiality law in the US), a reluctance to complicate the care situation by involving other parties, or another legitimate concern. Whatever the reason, once diagnosed with a dementing disorder, a patient is at increasing risk of negative outcomes over time. The patient may forget to take medications on time or at all; the patient may forget that driving privileges were suspended and continue to drive; the patient may fall victim to telemarketers or mail order scams and forfeit needed resources, and so on. Family members are typically (though not always) in the best position to monitor, guide, and protect persons with AD over time. It is usually best to find a way to communicate with and involve family in the care process whenever possible.

Referral to community services and resources can also be extremely helpful to families. In the US, the Alzheimer's Association provides informational support, respite care, and case management services, 24-hour helpline assistance, and support groups for the benefit of persons with dementia and family members alike. Area Agencies on Aging are another source of information and supportive services in many US cities. Similar organizations exist in other countries. The more resources and services a family can muster, the better their chances to cope effectively in the provision of dementia care over time.

Case example

John Doe is a 78-year-old, retired postal worker, with 12 years of education. He lives with his wife of 47 years, Doris, in a 2-bedroom home in small city in central US. Mr Doe and his wife have one child, a son, Paul, who lives 300 miles away. Paul is married with three children and manages a construction business. He is close to his parents emotionally, but rarely has time to visit or otherwise assist them. Mr Doe, a Korean War veteran, retired at age 65 years and spends a few days per week volunteering at the local Veterans of Foreign Wars (VFW) Hall. He is active at church and enjoys playing golf 2–3 times per week.

Over the past 18 months, Mrs Doe has become increasingly concerned about her husband's memory for recent events and information. He repeats himself regularly and has forgotten to follow through on commitments, only to deny later that he ever knew about them. At first, she attributed some of this behavior to his cantankerous personality – he just doesn't care about things as he used to – but her level of concern increased when he forgot his way home from the VFW Hall and drove for an hour before becoming oriented again. She convinced him to see his doctor following this incident on a pretense (a shoulder injury sustained while mowing the lawn needed attention), but with the intention of asking about his memory loss at the same time.

During the appointment with his primary care physician, Mr Doe acknowledged having some 'slight forgetfulness' but downplayed its significance. 'I'm getting older and I don't need to keep track of things as in the past. I'm doing just fine.' His physician, Dr Roberts, asked about depression or other stresses in his life. 'I have no such problems' was the reply. This was later confirmed by his wife. He also asked about history of memory loss in Mr Doe's family (his mother showed signs of dementia in her late 70s but was never diagnosed) and then decided to administer the MMSE. Mr Doe scored 23 of 30 points, missing items in orientation (incorrect month, date, and floor of the building), mental control (two errors in counting backwards by 7), and memory (only recalled 1 of 3 words after a brief delay).

Mr Doe was clearly surprised by his performance, but also somewhat incredulous: 'I'm sure I'll do better on that next time.'

Dr Roberts asked to speak with Mrs Doe separately and Mr Doe agreed. During this 5-minute interview, Mrs Doe told of her husband getting lost and an important commitment at the VFW Hall that he completely forgot. 'I've never known him to get lost or forget something like this. I'm really worried for him. I recall his mother having similar problems, but only now am I connecting things.' She reported that his memory was getting gradually worse over time. This information convinced Dr Roberts to order an MRI brain scan and laboratory tests to rule out an acute or reversible cause for his apparent cognitive dysfunction.

All medical tests and scans came back normal. Based on Mrs Doe's convincing report of gradual decline, and Mr Doe's errors on the MMSE, particularly in memory and orientation (two areas affected early in the course of clinical AD), Dr Roberts chose to make a diagnosis of probable mild AD and initiated drug therapy. He planned to follow Mr Doe closely and confirm this diagnostic impression over time.

Neither of the Does seemed surprised by the diagnosis, although Mr Doe didn't seem particularly concerned either. Mrs Doe expressed relief to 'finally know' why her husband was having problems. Dr Roberts referred them both to the Alzheimer's Association for education and support group assistance. He encouraged Mr Doe to continue in as many volunteer and other activities as he felt comfortable, but also asked Mrs Doe to monitor her husband's activities more closely. As a precaution, given that Mr Doe had become lost while driving, Dr Roberts also asked him to restrict his driving to daylight hours and familiar areas for now (thinking that a driving evaluation for safety reasons may be required sometime over the next year). A follow-up appointment was set up for 6 months hence.

Comment
The case of Mr Doe represents a fairly typical presentation of mild clinical AD: (1) memory loss and disorientation were gradually becoming a problem; (2) depression or unusual symptoms were not evident; (3) his wife reported clear examples of uncharacteristic failings; (4) there was a family history of dementia in his mother; and (5) he scored in the impaired range on a widely used screening test with errors consistent with historic report. This information was enough for Dr Roberts to make a diagnosis of probable mild AD and initiate drug therapy. His recommendations to stay active, monitor more closely, get involved with the Alzheimer's Association, begin restricting driving were consistent with Mr Doe's history and provided a structure for management in the future. Follow-up in 6 months would give Dr Roberts an opportunity to re-administer the MMSE, check on Mr Doe's response to medication, and lay the groundwork for future care.

With regards to driving and dementia, the American Academy of Neurology recommends that persons with mild dementia (CDR 1 level) stop driving for safety reasons (Dubinsky *et al.*, 2000). Dr Roberts is clearly aware of this recommendation, but chooses not to 'hit' the Does with it right away. Rather, he suggests a prudent restriction in driving exposure and lays the groundwork to revisit this issue in the coming months.

References

Alzheimer's Association (2004). 10 Warning Signs of Alzheimer's Disease. An on-line publication of the Alzheimer's Association: (http://www.alz.org/AboutAD/Warning.asp).

American Psychiatric Association (1994). *Diagnostic and Statistical Manual of Mental Disorders* (4th edn.). American Psychiatric Association, Washington.

Anstey KJ, Low LF (2004). Normal cognitive changes in aging. *Aus. Family Phys.* **33**:783–787.

Blessed G, Tomlinson BE, Roth M (1968). The association between quantitative measures of dementia and of senile change in the cerebral grey matter of elderly subjects. *Br. J. Psych.* **114**:797–811.

Brodaty H, Pond D, Kemp NM, *et al.* (2002). The GPCOG: a new screening test for dementia designed for general practice. *J. Am. Geriatric Soc.* **50**:530–534.

Buckles VD, Coats M, Morris JC (2000). *Best Practice of Medicine: Dementia.* Merck Medicus (http://merck.micromedex.com)

Chronic Care Networks for Alzheimer's Disease (2003). *Tools for early identification, assessment and treatment for people with Alzheimer's disease and dementia.* A publication of the Alzheimer's Association and National Chronic Care Consortium (http://www.alz.org/ Resources/FactSheets/CCN-AD03.pdf; page 9).

Connell CM, Janevic MR, Gallant MP (2001). The costs of caring: impact of dementia on family caregivers. *J. Geriatric Psych. Neurol.* **14**(4):179–187.

Costa PT, *et al.* (1996). *Clinical Practice Guideline, Quick Reference Guide for Clinicians* (No. 19), US Department of Health and Human Services, Rockville.

Davis P (2004). *The Long Goodbye: Memories of My Father.* Alfred A Knopf Publishing, New York.

DeBaggio T (2002). *Losing My Mind: An Intimate Look at Life with Alzheimer's,* The Free Press/Simon & Schuster, New York.

Dubinsky RM, Stein AC, Lyons K (2000). Practice parameter: risk of driving and Alzheimer's disease (an evidence-based review): Report of the Quality Standards Subcommittee of the American Academy of Neurology. *Neurology* **54**:2205–2211.

Folstein MF, *et al.* (1975). *J. Psych. Res.* **12**:189–198.

Hebert LE, Scherr PA, Bienias JL, *et al.* (2003). Alzheimer's disease in the US population: prevalence estimates using the 2000 census. *Arch. Neurol.* **60**:1119–1122.

Hughes CP, Berg L, Danziger WL, *et al.* (1982). A new clinical scale for the staging of dementia. *Br. J. Psych.* **140**:566–572.

Katzman R, Brown T, Fuld P, Peck A, Schechter R, Schimmel H (1983). Validation of a short Orientation-Memory-Concentration test of cognitive impairment. *Am. J. Psych.* **140**:734–739.

Kawas CH (2003). Early Alzheimer's disease. *N. Engl. J. Med.* **349**:1056–1063.

Keefover RW (1990). Alzheimer's disease as a diagnosis of exclusion. *W. Virginia Med. J.* **86**(2):51–55.

Knopman DS, DeKosky ST, Cummings JL, *et al.* (2001). Practice parameter: diagnosis of dementia (an evidence-based review). Report of the Quality Standards Subcommittee of the American Academy of Neurology. *Neurology* **56**(9):1143–1153.

Meuser TM, Boise L, Morris JC (2004). Clinician beliefs and practice in dementia care: implications for health educators. *Ed. Geront.* **30**:491–516.

Marwit SJ, Meuser TM (2002). Development and initial validation of an inventory to assess grief in caregivers of persons with Alzheimer's disease. *Gerontologist* **42**(6):751–765.

Meuser TM, Marwit SJ (2001). A comprehensive, stage-sensitive model of grief in dementia caregiving. *Gerontologist* **41**(5):658–700.

Morris JC (1993). The Clinical Dementia Rating (CDR): current version and scoring rules. *Neurology* **43**:2412–2414.

Murphy DD, Ravina B (2003). Brain banking for neurodegenerative diseases. *Curr. Opin. Neurol.* **16**(4):459–463.

National Institutes of Health (1987). Differential diagnosis of dementing diseases: NIH Consensus Statement. *JAMA* **258**(23):3411–3416.

Pastor P, Goate AM (2004). Molecular genetics of Alzheimer's disease. *Curr. Psych. Reports* **6**(2):125–133.

Petersen RC, Stevens JC, Ganguli M, *et al.* (2001). Practice parameter: early detection of dementia: mild cognitive impairment (an evidence-based review). Report of the Quality Standards Subcommittee of the American Academy of Neurology. *Neurology* **56**(9):1133–1142.

Reisberg B, Ferris SH, de Leon MJ, *et al.* (1982). Global Deterioration Scale. *Am. J. Psych.* **139**:1136–1139.

Small GW, Rabins PV, Barry PP, *et al.* (1997). Diagnosis and treatment of Alzheimer disease and related disorders. Consensus statement of the American Association for Geriatric Psychiatry, the Alzheimer's Association, and the American Geriatrics Society. *JAMA* **278**:1363–1371.

Solomon PR, Pendlebury WW (1998). Recognition of Alzheimer's disease: the 7 Minute Screen. *Family Med.* **30**:265–271.

Chapter 3

Diagnosis of Alzheimer's disease: neuropathologic investigation methods

Introduction

This chapter describes protocols used to establish definitive pathological diagnoses using autopsy central nervous system (CNS) material from demented subjects. The presentation is divided into four parts: (1) the autopsy procedures for obtaining brain, spinal cord, cerebrospinal fluid (CSF), and pituitary gland specimens; (2) the diagnostic algorithm used to distinguish brains with healthy aging changes from those with pure or mixed dementing disorders; and (3) the histologic and immunohistochemical (IHC) methods that were used in Washington University's Alzheimer's Disease Research Center (ADRC) from 1986 to 2004 in order to assign final neuropathologic diagnoses on primary and secondary causes of dementia. Part 4 describes emerging diagnostic methods that materially add to knowledge of pathogenic mechanisms of dementing disorders.

Establishing a histopathologic baseline for normality is a necessary task in order to assess the presence or absence of the burgeoning multiplicity of dementing diseases, which is the main focus of Part 2. In the case of nondemented controls, the primary goals of postmortem brain examination are to study: (1) any incidental pathologic changes; (2) brain lesions due to aging *per se*, and (3) to assess the possible presence of preclinical pathologic aging-related Alzheimer's disease (AD). The specific neuropathologic findings associated with these three categories of changes in cognitively intact control brains are more fully described in Chapters 4 and 5.

Part 3 provides a practical rationale the ADRC uses for specific dye and immunohistochemical techniques used to study the healthy aging brain and to diagnose AD and the non-AD dementing disorders and their preclinical forms.

Removing and processing the brain, spinal cord, pituitary gland, and cerebrospinal fluid at autopsy

Autopsy protocol

The following protocols are those required by the state of Missouri, US. Since 1999, mentally competent persons have been able to sign their own autopsy permits. Separate autopsy permission from family members after death is not necessary. Other persons must have an autopsy permit signed after death by the legal next-of-kin according to a hierarchy of relationships (e.g. from the Missouri autopsy statutes, website URL: http://www.moga.state.mo.us/statutes/C100-199/1940000115.htm). Research subjects whose brain or other postmortem tissues or bodily fluids will be used for genetic analyses must also agree to and sign a Genetics Consent document that is approved by the Institutional Review Board (IRB). Genetic analyses related to dementing disorders might include apolipoprotein E (apoE) allele genotyping of DNA, or DNA sequencing to define etiologic mutations for AD (Bertram & Tanzi, 2004), Parkinson's disease (PD) (Forman *et al.*, 2005a), or various tauopathies (Rademakers *et al.*, 2004).

Reviewing clinical data

The clinical history available to the neuropathologist at the time of death includes the following: (1) current and past hospital medical charts; (2) information on the 'Clinical Abstract' portion of the autopsy permission form that includes the suspected clinical cause/s of death and any special features that need to be investigated; (3) information from the postmortem dementia assessment conducted by ADRC nurse coordinators; and (4) research information contained in an on-line 'Autopsy Database'. The latter ADRC-wide resource, a subset of information in the main SAS Institute, Cary, NC database, is accessed over secure virtual private network connections that utilize a user identity, password, and data encryption to comply with Health Insurance Portability and Accountability Act regulations. The Autopsy Database information includes: the Clinical Dementia Rating (CDR) (Hughes *et al.*, 1982; Morris, 1993) or CDR at the last clinical assessment; the year of dementia onset (from which the total duration of dementia can be readily calculated); the final clinical diagnoses of the underlying cause/s of dementia; the date, place and time of death; and known current medications. The postmortem interval (PMI) can then be calculated as the time interval in fractional hours (e.g. 9.2) that elapsed between pronouncement of death and CSF or brain tissue collection and storage at -80°C or fixation in 10% (commercial) neutral buffered formalin (10% NBF). Criteria are currently being finalized by several national committees to define a standard set of agonal factors to be recorded by all ADRCs at the time of death (see Appendix for details of the National Alzheimer's Coordinating Center [NACC]). The ADRC Neuropathology Core Leaders and their Quality Assurance and Standards subcommittee are considering standard methods to assess brain tissue integrity at the time of death. Such measures might include assessment of brain pH and Western blot analysis to assess messenger ribonucleic acid (mRNA) yield and quality (Kingsbury *et al.*, 1995).

Postmortem CSF, brain and pituitary removal and processing

At the time of autopsy a scalpel is used to incise the scalp, being careful to reflect the skull and not cut the hair. A reciprocating saw is used to detach the dome of the skull and a triangular notch is cut in the frontal bone to stabilize the position of the 'skull cap' once it is replaced. Both outer and inner surfaces of the dura are inspected after being 'stripped' by the autopsy assistants. Any sites of bleeding, trauma to the scalp and soft tissues, or skull fractures are recorded on autopsy forms. This part of the brain examination is important, particularly in elderly persons who are either at risk for falling or have fallen (often many times). Falls are common in AD and dementia with Lewy body (DLB) patients in particular. The brain is then accessible for CSF collection, brain and pituitary removal, frozen tissue collection, and chemical fixation.

Postmortem CSF collection

The falx cerebri is removed with scissors and forceps and the the two medial surfaces of the cerebral hemispheres are gently separated to expose the junction of the anterior and middle thirds of the corpus callosum (CC), the target site for withdrawing CSF (**3.1**). One hand is stabilized by resting firmly on the frontal bone and the beveled needle tip of a sterile, disposable long spinal tap needle is inserted just

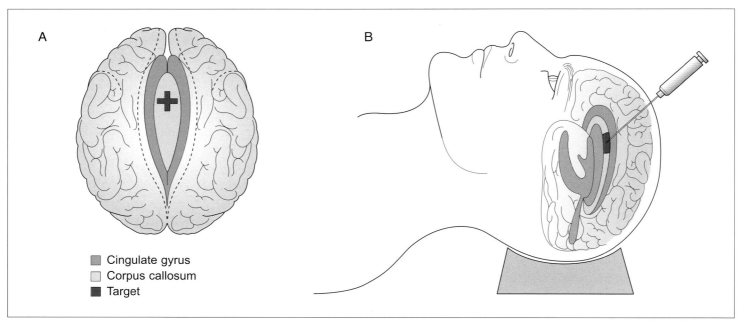

- Cingulate gyrus
- Corpus callosum
- Target

3.1 A Location for withdrawing cerebrospinal fluid at autopsy from the exposed cerebrum after removing the skull cap. The needle, positioned as shown in (**B**), is inserted at the junction of the exposed anterior 1/3 and posterior 2/3rds of the corpus callosum at a 45° angle. The bevel of the needle is just below the inferior border of the corpus callosum.

beneath the CC. The goal is to withdraw 30 ml of CSF. Obtaining this amount of fluid is often possible in moderately and severely demented persons with advanced cerebral atrophy and dilated cerebral ventricles. However, experience with over 300 nondemented and demented autopsy cases indicates that the amount of CSF obtained with the initial attempt is usually all that is possible. Further attempts at collecting additional CSF volume often lead to outright failure, or obtaining CSF contaminated with blood or brain tissue fragments. Failures on 'second attempt' CSF collection from cadavers is due either to the cerebral ventricles not being enlarged or to collapse of the ventricles during CSF removal. Collected postmortem CSF (pmCSF) is first placed in a 100 ml sterile plastic urine cup on ice. Aliquots (2 ml) are then placed into 15 prelabeled, screw-capped, low temperature cryotubes and frozen at -80°C without further treatment. The volume and clarity of the collected pmCSF is recorded on a standard data form.

As far as use of pmCSF for clinicopathologic research, initial experiments have shown that postmortem proteolysis causes severe artifactual elevations in phosphorylated tau in pmCSF, with four separate antibodies, that invalidates this measurement (Morihara *et al.*, 1998; DW McKeel, Jr & P Davies, unpublished data). On the other hand, measurement of pmCSF beta-amyloid levels may be possible as this protein appears to be more stable after death (Strozyk *et al.*, 2003).

Brain removal and initial processing for histologic examination, diagnostic and research IHC and biochemical analysis

Once pmCSF has been collected and placed on ice, the dural attachments along the lateral surfaces of the cerebral hemispheres and the tentorium cerebelli are detached using a number 11 (sharp pointed) scalpel blade, being careful to avoid incising the brain. Next the olfactory bulbs and tracts are dislodged gently from the cribriform plate and are reflected backwards for subsequent harvesting. The surgical scalpel and number 11 blade are used to cut both optic nerves at the optic foramina and to sever the internal carotid arteries (ICAs) as they exit the cavernous sinus on either side of the sella turcica containing the pituitary gland. Scissors occasionally may be required to cut through heavily calcified ICAs. Each cranial nerve is then cut as close to the skull base as possible. Once the tentorium has been incised and the brain stem exposed, the vertebral arteries can be

identified and cut using a long-handled #3 scalpel handle with a number 11 blade. For 'brain only' limited brain autopsy cases especially, it is important to sever the spinal cord as far down in the foramen magnum as possible using the same instrument.

Examination of the spinal cord is frequently neglected in neurodegenerative disorders despite growing evidence in the literature that this structure is involved in several dementing disorders (Kato *et al.*, 1992; Holton *et al.*, 2001).

Removal of the entire spinal cord at autopsy

Using a standard anterior approach after the organ block has been removed, the anterior vertebral bodies are removed *en bloc* with a reciprocating saw. The cord and dura with attached dorsal and ventral nerve roots and dorsal root ganglia should be removed as a whole. The spinal dura should be opened along its entire length to allow removal of segments to be snap frozen and to allow uniform exposure of the cord to 10% NBF for optimal histopathologic examination.

Removal and fixation of the pituitary at autopsy

Once the brain has been removed, the dural diaphragma sellae is circumferentially incised with a number 11 scalpel blade on a #3 long handle to expose the hypophysis (pituitary gland). Smooth tipped forceps are used to grasp a dural edge and the gland is removed using gentle traction and sharp dissection. The gland is then bivalved in the mid-horizontal plane using a Pathco™ double edged surgical knife and blade after it is weighed to the tenth of a gram (**3.2**, overleaf). Normal mean pituitary weight obtained in this manner for adults is about 0.6–0.7 g with a range of 0.3–0.7 g being normal for elderly adults who die after 70 years of age. The gland halves are placed in a regular tissue cassette and fixed for 2 days in 10% NBF. Paraffin sections (5 μm) are examined with hematoxylin eosin (H&E) to visualize cytologic features of the stalk, neurohypophysis, 'invading adrenocorticotropic hormone (ACTH) basophils' of the posterior lobe, the glandular pars tuberalis surrounding the pituitary stalk, the pars intermedia residual Rathke pouch follicular glands, and the adenohypophyseal red eosinophil classic growth hormone-secreting acidophils, the classic ACTH-secreting basophils (high granular affinity for hematoxylin with a large vacuole), and secretory cells with poorly granulated, faintly staining cytoplasm, the classic anterior pituitary chromophobes (Fowler & McKeel, 1979a, b).

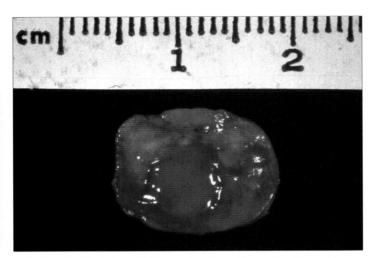

3.2 One-half of the pituitary gland sectioned in the mid-horizontal plane parallel to the skull base shows a central, gelatinous appearing adenoma. The surrounding adenohypophysis (AP) is a variegated orange color. The neurohypophysis (NP) is the elliptical white structure at the top center of the hypophysis. One large pars intermedia follicle is visible as a dark area between the center of the AP and the NP.

The rationale for examining the pituitary gland in dementia cases rests on the following data: (1) screening for hypothyroidism is frequently done to rule out this treatable and hence reversible cause of dementia. The anterior pituitary gland shows thyroid stimulating hormone (TSH) (thyrotrope) hypertrophy, hyperplasia, and adenoma formation in cases of untreated hypothyoidsim (Horvath *et al.*, 1999); (2) dopaminergic deficits (e.g. as occur in PD) may be reflected by release of tonic dopaminergic inhibition of anterior pituitary prolactin cells leading to prolactin cell hyperplasia and hyperprolactinemia (Bellomo *et al.*, 1991); and (3) systemic disorders that produce cardiovascular signs and symptoms all cause ischemic lesions in the pituitary gland. Some examples of these disorders include diabetes mellitus (Watson & Craft, 2003), myocardial infarction, bilateral carotid strokes, and head trauma.

Most endocrine system disorders are reflected in pituitary gland cytomorphology. This type of information may be a useful adjunct in assessing the degree of involvement of the endocrine hypothalamus when a dementing disorder affects this crucial brain region (e.g. AD where plaques and tangles are common). Corroboration of diabetes mellitus may be obtained by observing lymphocytes in the pars intermedia,

ACTH hyperplasia, and scattered stellate ischemic scars (healed microinfarcts) in the adenohypophysis. Such lesions are common in pituitary glands from insulin-requiring diabetics (Flynn *et al.*, 1988).

Examination of peripheral nerve and muscle tissue in dementia cases

The importance of examining clinically affected skeletal muscle and peripheral nerve in non-AD dementias cannot be overemphasized. The need to do so in classical lower motor neuron diseases (MND) with advanced muscle atrophy such as amyotrophic lateral sclerosis (ALS) is obvious. However, clinical signs of MND in frontotemporal dementia (FTD) disorders may be very subtle, initially consisting of muscle fasciculations detectable only by electromyographic methods and mild deficits in nerve conduction velocities (de Carvalho, 2001).

Morphologic data on spinal cord, peripheral nerves and skeletal muscle are sorely lacking in the FTD-MND disorders. Examination of skeletal muscle may be especially rewarding as some 'muscle diseases' show accumulation of the same two proteins, beta amyloid and hyperphosphorylated tau, that characterize AD senile plaques and neurofibrillary tangles (Vattemi *et al.*, 2003). Muscle and nerve changes may be part of hereditary dementing disorders as well (fragile-X carriers) (Forman *et al.*, 2005b).

Autopsy techniques for examining skeletal muscle and peripheral nerve
Techniques for examining human sural nerve and skeletal muscle biopsies (Kanda *et al.*, 1996) may be applied to human postmortem specimens.

Examining peripheral nerve samples
Portions of the sural nerve should be frozen, placed in neutral buffered glutaraldehyde electron microscopy (EM) fixative, and a third segment fixed in 10% NBF for routine diagnostic evaluation. Nerve fiber 'tease' preparations are valuable for assessing segmental demyelinating processes and axonal loss, for example as occurs in diabetic neuropathy. Luxol fast blue-periodic acid-Schiff (PAS, the Klüver–Barrera stain; Klüver & Barrera, 1953; Luna, 1968) and impregnation with osmium tetroxide ('osmic acid') are useful for studying such preparations. Nerve specimens embedded in EM plastics, cut at 0.5–1.0 μm, and stained

with toluidine blue are highly informative for assessing both myelinated and unmyelinated nerve fibers at high resolution, fiber density, and size distribution at the light microscopic level. Schwann cells, fibroblasts, and inflammatory cells can be easily identified with greater diagnostic certainty than is the case for thicker paraffin sections.

Examining skeletal muscle samples

Skeletal muscle samples should include appropriate clinically-affected muscles. Autopsy muscle samples can be fixed in a muscle surgical biopsy clamp; however, good morphologic preservation still can be obtained if one is not available. Muscle samples, similar to peripheral nerve, should be fixed in 10% NBF for histopathologic examination. An additional muscle sample also should be snap frozen in liquid nitrogen to facilitate muscle immunohistochemistry and biochemistry. Both cross sections and longitudinal sections of skeletal muscle should be examined. This is required to detect subtle early changes. Plastic-embedded skeletal muscle specimens (1 µm) are useful for studying muscle fiber size and shape, fiber inclusions, and the nature of infiltrating cells. For example, subtle morphologic changes such as fiber angulation, a prelude to group fiber atrophy, help to diagnose early ALS–MND (Troost et al., 1992).

Washington University ADRC algorithm for diagnosing AD and non-AD dementias as distinct from healthy brain aging

Neuropathologists face several distinct challenges in assessing postmortem brains for a histopathologic diagnosis of AD. These hurdles include: (1) a lack of standardized criteria for diagnosing preclinical pathologic AD; (2) confusion in the literature between mild cognitive impairment (MCI) (Petersen, 2004) and very mild AD as defined by the CDR (McKeel et al., 1993; Kirshner, 2005); and (3) lack of comprehensive information about cognitive status near the time of death. Another difficulty is interpreting co-occurring dementing disorders such as small vascular infarcts with respect to their contribution to the overall degree of cognitive impairment.

This chapter will first consider each of these challenges and will emphasize diagnostically useful neuropathologic methods. It will then suggest an algorithmic approach to AD

diagnosis, developed to classify AD and co-occurring neurodegenerative disorders efficiently.

The algorithm currently used evolved from a diagnostic protocol for various dementing disorders that was proposed by Lowe (1998). Several reviews and monographs that cover the full spectrum of neurodegenerative disorders include those by Markesbery (1998), Esiri and colleagues (1997; 2004), and an International Society of Neuropathology monograph edited by Dickson (2003).

Figure **3.3** (overleaf) includes the diagnostic algorithm currently in use at the author's medical center and ADRC for classifying AD and non-AD dementing disorders. This scheme has evolved during the accession of more than 1,020 brains that were collected between 1981 and mid-2004. A number of studies have now been published (Crystal et al., 1988; Katzman et al., 1988; Morris et al., 1996) showing that a significant minority of clinically assessed nondemented persons have AD pathology on brain autopsy, now defined as 'preclinical pathologic AD'. There is some confusion about the use of the term 'preclinical' at both the clinical and pathologic levels. Some investigators apply preclinical only to persons whose cognition is completely intact (i.e. CDR 0), assessed by the most stringent methods including the use of a close collateral source. Other investigators use the term to refer to persons who do not meet formal Alzheimer's Disease and Related Disorders Association (ADRDA) (Blackwell et al., 2004) or DSM-III or -IV criteria for dementia, even though there are subtle cognitive impairments.

None of the existing standardized diagnostic methods based on histopathology are entirely adequate for diagnosing preclinical or very mild (CDR 0.5) pathologic AD. Cognitive profiles of a CDR 0.5 group of patients studied by the author overlap with individuals described in the literature as having MCI (Grundman et al., 2004; Desai & Grossberg, 2005). Indeed, 70% of CDR 0.5/MCI overlap patients progress to overt CDR 1 AD within 2 years (Goldman et al., 2001). Some key features that differentiate the three main diagnostic schemes for AD are presented in Table 3.1 (overleaf). For convenience in the following paragraphs the author will refer to total (diffuse and neuritic) senile plaques (TSP), diffuse senile plaques (DSP) and neuritic senile plaques (NSP).

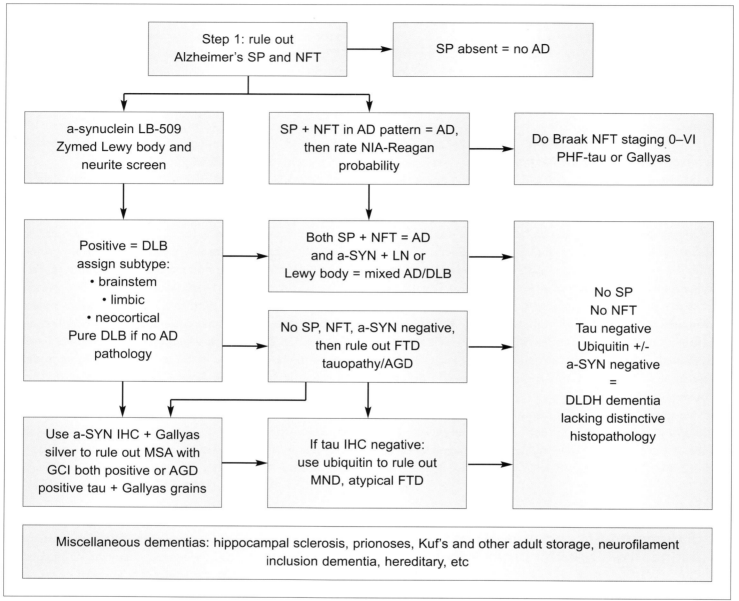

3.3 Flow diagram to show the diagnostic schema followed at the author's center to make a pathologic diagnosis of specific dementing disorders. Alzheimer's disease is first ruled in or out, then Lewy diseases, then tauopathies, frontotemporal dementias and miscellaneous disorders, such as prion-related diseases.

Table 3.1 Neuropathologic diagnosis of Alzheimer's disease: 3 leading sets of criteria

Criteria	Age-adjusted	Main features	Citation
NIA-Khachaturian	Yes	Neocortex total plaques (diffuse and neuritic)	Khachaturian (1985)
CERAD	Yes	Cortex neuritic plaques only	Mirra *et al.* (1991)
NIA–Reagan Institute	No	Neuritic plaques only; Braak NFP staging	NIA–Reagan (1997); Braak and Braak (1991)

CERAD: Consortium to Establish a Registry for Alzheimer's Disease; NFP: neurofibrillary pathology (tangles, neuropil threads, senile plaque neurites)

The National Institute on Aging (NIA) (Khachaturian, 1985) criteria

The National Institute on Aging (NIA) (Khachaturian, 1985) criteria are based on the age-adjusted density (number per mm^2) of diffuse and neuritic senile plaques (TSP) in any area of the prefrontal, temporal, parietal, or medial occipital neocortex. These criteria are the only ones that are quantitative. The higher the age at death, the higher the threshold for plaque density (*Table 3.2*). The presence of some neocortical tangles is required up to age 75 years but not thereafter. A built-in feature (often overlooked) is thus recognition of the fact that overall plaque and tangle burden may be less in the very elderly, a point that has been established by independent studies (Giannakopoulos *et al.*, 1996; Berg *et al.*, 1998).

Currently, the original Khachaturian 1985 NIA consensus criteria have been supplanted by the newer NIA-Reagan Institute criteria (1997). The primary reasons for this included a feeling among some investigators that plaque quantification was too difficult reliably across CERAD diagnostic centers (Mirra *et al.*, 1994). Also, the 1997 NIA-Reagan Working Group believed that the addition of tangle-based scoring using the Braak and Braak (1991a) system would add to the usefulness of the criteria. A recent study, building on previous Washington University ADRC data (McKeel *et al.*, 1993), showed that modified Khachaturian diagnostic criteria provide the highest available sensitivity and specificity for distinguishing between pure (i.e. no co-morbid dementing disorders) nondemented cognitively normal CDR 0 controls and pure clinical AD (McKeel *et al.*, 2004).

The Consortium to Establish a Registry for Diagnosing AD (CERAD) criteria

This North American consortium of 28 participating Alzheimer centers developed a new set of pathologic criteria for diagnosing AD in 1991 in an effort to facilitate sharing of case information reliably across multiple centers (Mirra *et al.*, 1991). NSP were used as the primary lesion in the belief that this type of 'mature' plaque had a greater effect, compared to 'benign' DSP, in disrupting neuronal pathways and causing dementia. An age-adjusted NSP score was generated based on the maximum number of NSP detected in any of the four neocortical lobes. The number of tangles was also scored semi-quantitatively, yet this assessment did not enter into the final diagnosis. Senile plaque (SP) and neurofibrillary tangle (NFT) lesion scoring was facilitated by reference to cartoons showing 2, 6, and 28 NSP or NFT as equivalent to 'mild', 'moderate', and 'severe'. This implied the build-up of both SP and NFT was curvilinear and not linear with time. This function was not stipulated in the 1991 paper nor was it fitted to any experimental data.

Table 3.2 NIA-Khachaturian 1985 age-adjusted criteria for diagnosing Alzheimer's disease

'Minimum microscopic criteria' (per single 1 sq mm field neocortex)	
Below 50 years	2–5 SP *and* NFT
50 to 65 years	≥ 8 SP + some NFT
66 to 75 years	≥10 SP + some NFT
Over 75 years	≥15 SP ± some NFT

(Khachaturian, 1985)

The NIA-Reagan Institute criteria for diagnosing AD

The CERAD neuritic SP scoring system was incorporated into the 1997 NIA–Reagan Institute criteria and thus survives. Thus, an NSP score is first obtained and then a Braak NFP score is assigned to arrive at a probability score for that brain having pathologic AD as 'low', 'moderate' (or intermediate), or 'high'.

NIA–Reagan Institute criteria were developed to assess pathologic lesions including senile plaques and neurofibrillary tangles in demented brains only. Thus, the criteria by *definition* are not suitable to assess preclinical pathologic AD. By this system most CDR 0.5 subjects who have definite pathologic criteria by modified Khachaturian criteria have 'low probability' AD by NIA–Reagan Institute pathologic criteria. Research performed at the author's ADRC convincingly demonstrates that abundant neocortical DSP with some NSP are the best marker for the onset of very early AD (Morris & Price, 2001). For this reason, the author continues to stress the overall utility of Washington University ADRC modified Khachaturian criteria for the full spectrum of AD pathology ranging from none (CDR 0) to preclinical disease and later stages of very mild (CDR 0.5), mild (CDR 1), moderately severe (CDR 2), and severe (CDR 3) clinical AD. The original and Washington University modified Khachaturian NIA consensus diagnostic criteria quantify both DSP and NSP. In doing so, these criteria do acknowledge that some neocortical NFTs are intrinsic to AD pathogenesis. Of interest, the cut-points defined for the Washington University ADRC modified Khachaturian criteria (McKeel *et al.*, 2004) fall precisely in the plaque density range designated in the original publication (Khachaturian, 1985) (*Box 3.1*).

Box 3.1 Neuropathologic core features of dementing disorders

Core criteria for diagnosing AD
- Very mild, preclinical: neocortical widespread diffuse SP, rare NFT (Braak I–III)
- Mild to severe: increasing cortical NSP, NFT, NT (Braak III–VI)

Core criteria for diagnosing DLB
- DLB brainstem (brainstem > 5/section; limbic, cortical CLB <5/section)
- DLB limbic (limbic > CLB 5/section; cortical <5/section, most brainstem >5)
- DLB neocortical (cortex CLB >5/section)

Core criteria for diagnosing FTD
- Frontal and/or temporal lobar atrophy
- Severe lobar neuronal loss
- Severe lobar gliosis (with neuron loss)
- Superficial cortical microvacuolation
- Tau+ neuronal and glial inclusions in gray matter and white matter, variable (DLDH none)

Core criteria for diagnosing VaD
- Three or more infarcts c/w dementia duration (disregard acute)
- Presence of recognized ischemic pathology: arterio/atherosclerosis, CAA, cortical laminar necrosis, chronic hemorrhages, recurrent strokes
- Elevated Hachinski score >7

AD: Alzheimer's disease; CAA: cerebral amyloid angiopathy; CLB: cortical Lewy body; DLB: dementia with Lewy body; DLDH: dementia lacking distinctive histopathology; FTD: frontotemporal dementia; NFT: neurofibrillary tangle; NSP: neuritic senile plaque; NT: neuropil thread; VaD: vascular dementia

Histologic dyes and IHC, antibody-based methods

Conventional dye methods

Methods described here are generally useful for assessing the full spectrum of neurodegenerative disorders in adults: H&E, Nissl methods for neurons, thioflavine S, Congo red, luxol fast blue (LFB)- PAS, modified Bielschowsky silver (20% silver nitrate), Hedreen–Bielschowsky silver (4% cupric nitrate, 4% silver nitrate), and Gallyas silver.

Hematoxylin and eosin

This venerable histopathologic general screening stain has many 'flavors'. The use of eosin preparations with too much red obscure many diagnostic features that define neurodegenerative disorders (SP, Lewy bodies). Eosin solutions containing phloxine have proven to be optimal in the author's hands. Hematoxylin is a complex dye mixture that is 'blued' by running tap water. A robust intense blue that allows the full color range of eosin to be appreciated is the desired staining effect.

Recognition of pathognomonic inclusions that define dementing disorders using H&E may be difficult except in the case of classical haloed Lewy bodies. The H&E protocol the author uses (see Appendix) also gives excellent discrimination for hippocampal granulovacuoles and Hirano bodies, cortical Lewy bodies, a subset of SPs, and intraneuronal and extracellular NFTs. This method is highly recommended to diagnose dementing disorders and is illustrated throughout this book. Other dye stains are useful in defining human normal and pathologic neuroanatomy as shown (**3.4**).

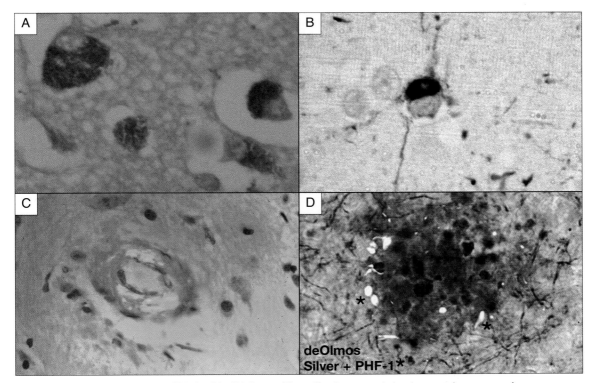

3.4 A: Ballooned neurons filled with PAS-positive diastase-resistant granular secondary lysosomes in a case of adult ceroid lipofuscinosis (×40 objective). **B**: Cortical Lewy body and associated neurites labeled by alpha synuclein antibody (×40 objective). **C**: Apple-green birefringence of a beta-amyloid-containing cerebral artery that has been stained with Congo red and is viewed with cross polarizing filters (×10 objective). **D**: Fluorescently tagged antibody to PHF tau (white boutons) that differ from the argyrophilic swollen neurites of a neuritic senile plaque that has been stained by the de Olmos silver method (×60 objective oil immersion).

Nissl staining for neurons

Classical neuroanatomists still make frequent use of relatively thick (40–50 μm) frozen sections of cryoprotected aldehyde-fixed human brains for assessing neuronal populations. Toluidine blue and cresyl echt violet are the dyes of choice. The crucial factor of a successful Nissl protocol is to obtain a crystal clear background. For example, in neuronal stereology, it is critical to be able to see nuclear membranes and nucleoli clearly. The protocol used at the Washington University ADRC was developed in the laboratory of Dr Joseph L Price to map AD lesions on large (50 μm) frozen brain sections (Morris & Price, 2001).

Thioflavine S

Thioflavines are a family of fluorescent dyes (thioflavine S and T are most often used in pathology laboratories) that are economical and effective in visualizing AD lesions such as SP, NFT, and cerebral amyloid angiopathy (CAA), as an adjunct to H&E screening (**3.5**) (Delacourte *et al.*, 1987; Vickers *et al.*, 2003). Lesions are moderately to intensely green-yellow fluorescent against a pale background of neuropil. The specific lesions of AD are easily distinguished from the orange autofluorescence of lipofuscin that accumulates in many human neurons as part of the normal aging process (Porta, 2002).

Thioflavine S is also widely used to assess 'fibrillar' b-amyloid plaques in transgenic amyloid precursor protein (APP) mice (Games *et al.*, 1991; Brendza *et al.*, 2003). The results of plaque staining in transgenic mice that overexpress a-beta protein differ in some important respects from human AD amyloid deposits. For example, most of the diffuse neocortical amyloid 'plaques' in PDAPP mice are

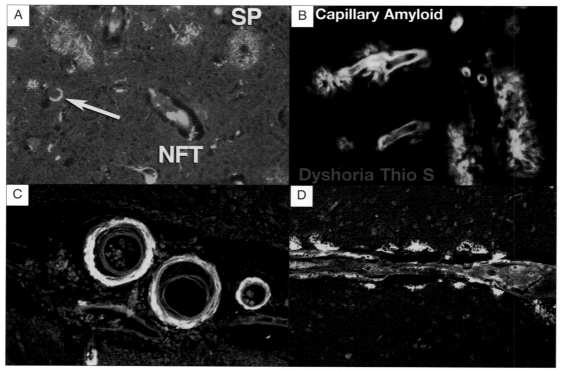

3.5 Thioflavine S stained 6 μm paraffin sections viewed by epifluoresence with a fluorescein type filter. **A**: Fluorescent senile plaques (SP), neurofibrillary tangles (NFT), and neuronal cytoplasmic lipofuscin (arrow) in the cortex of an advanced Alzheimer patient (×20 objective). **B**: Beta-amyloid-containing cerebral capillaries, some with spike-like projections (dyshoria), in longitudinal and cross-sectional views (×40 objective). **C**: Leptomeningeal arteries, two of which have double lumens that are caused by mural deposition of beta-amyloid (×10 objective). **D**: Dyshoric reaction of a small cerebral artery with segmental involvement of the wall by beta-amyloid (×10 objective).

thioflavine S-negative in contrast to the thioflavine S-*positive* earliest diffuse beta-amyloid plaques that accumulate in Down's (trisomy 21) syndrome brains from affected individuals who die in their teens and 20s (**3.6**). A likely explanation is that thioflavine S-negative amyloid deposits conform to human 'preamyloid plaques'. These early plaque forms were defined by Tagliavini *et al.* (1988) as plaques that immunolabel with a-beta antibodies but are negative using silver methods, Congo red and thioflavine S.

Thioflavine S also dramatically highlights neuronal lipopigment in the adult form of Kuf's ceroid lipofuscinosis storage disease (**3.7**) (Josephson *et al.*, 2001). Affected neurons are ballooned and the cytoplasm is filled with intensely fluorescent granular deposits. Lewy bodies are generally only faintly positive with thioflavine stains and Lewy neurites are not stained. The tauopathy lesions of FTD cases, unlike AD tangles, are mostly silver-, Congo red- (see below), and thioflavine S-negative. Straight filament tangles in PSP are thioflavine S-negative and Bielschowsky silver-positive.

Congo red

Congo red (CR) is the classic dye staining 'gold standard' method for histologically defining the entire family of amyloidoses. The common feature of all amyloids, systemic and localized, is the presence of a high content of beta-pleated sheet substructure. CR dye molecules intercalate into molecular 'slots' formed by the beta-pleated sheets and thereby define a true amyloid protein as being CR-positive and exhibiting apple-green birefringence under polarized illumination. SP cores, NFTs and CAA (see **3.4C**) all exhibit this property.

Luxol fast blue-periodic acid Schiff

LFB-PAS has become the favorite stain for assessing brain myelin integrity in neuropathology laboratories around the world. The term 'Klüver–Barrera stain' (Akiguchi *et al.*, 2004) is synonymous. Intact myelin is stained an intense aqua blue color in contrast to demyelinated areas which are a paler blue color (**3.8**). The PAS component of LFB-PAS is useful for defining corpora amylacea, a subset

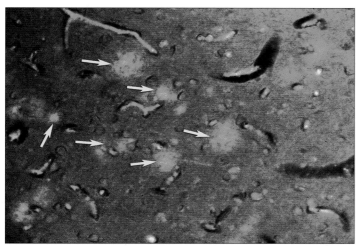

3.6 Multiple fluorescent diffuse Alzheimer beta amyloid plaques (arrows) are revealed by the thioflavine S technique in the cerebral cortex of a 24-year-old nondemented (CDR 0) woman who had trisomy 21 Down's syndrome. No tau-immunoreactive pathology was evident anywhere in this brain, and the plaques lacked tau-positive dystrophic neurites. The plaques also stained with the Hedreen–Bielschowsky method (×10 objective).

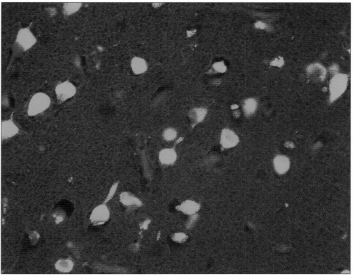

3.7 Thioflavine S method clearly reveals widespread swollen neocortical neurons which show massive pathologic accumulation of cytoplasmic lipopigment granules. Adult ceroid lipofuscinosis (Kuf's disease) patient (×40 objective, epifluorescent illumination).

of AD senile plaques, lipofuscin and ceroid granules, vascular basement membranes, gitter cell macrophage granules, and coarse granules in perivascular cells (pericytes, resting microglia).

Modified Bielshowsky silver stains

Dr Alois Alzheimer used Dr Bielschowsky's 1896 axonal silver method for defining senile plaques and neurofibrillary in the first reported case of AD in 1907. The diagnostic usefulness of this stain for diagnosing AD and displaying axons is thus well established and continuing. The Washington University ADRC Neuropathology Core laboratory has developed two variations that are useful for assessing NFTs and NSPs (see modified Bielschowsky silver protocol in the Appendix; 20% silver nitrate) and for total diffuse and neuritic SP using computer image analysis (Hibbard *et al.*, 1994; Cullen *et al.*, 1996) (see Hedreen–Bielschowsky silver in the Appendix; 4% cupric nitrate–4% silver nitrate). The different results obtained with the two methods are shown in figure **3.9**.

A great deal has been written about the relative merits of traditional silver methods versus IHC antibody-based methods for assessing AD plaques and tangles. Experience with parallel use of both methods over 15 years at the author's ADRC indicates that both silver and IHC methods are complementary. Each type of methodology has its own merits and pitfalls. It is often stated that silver methods are 'unreliable' or 'capricious' (and therefore not very useful in a modern setting). Yet silver methods work on archival brains stored for decades in formalin. Silver staining quality can be optimized by using fresh reagents and scrupulously clean acid-washed glassware. Under such conditions, these two silver methods are as reliable as antibody-based methods that have their own limitations. Figure **3.10** illustrates silver and IHC results in staining AD brain sections to assess SP and NFT. Washington University ADRC unpublished data (DW McKeel, Jr, K Powlishta, and NS Havlioglu) demonstrate both methods produce statistically comparable SP density counts, whereas tau immunostaining demonstrates elevated tangle counts due to pretangles that are not visualized with silver methods.

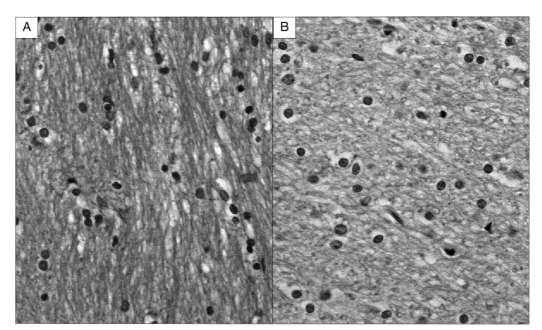

3.8 Kluver–Barrera luxol fast blue-periodic acid Schiff stain is a mainstay for examining myelin pathology. Normal myelin (**A**) stains uniformly blue. The nuclei belong to white matter oligodendrocytes and astrocytes (larger and clearer nuclei). In contrast, damaged myelin in **B** exhibits less intense nonuniform blue staining. Myelin has a circular, segmented pattern that differs from the more linear pattern of normal myelin sheaths. Such pathologically altered myelin would appear to be 'pale' in H&E screening sections (×20 objective).

While monoclonal antibodies (mabs) are said to be '100% specific' for their antigen, practical experience indicates that multiple dissimilar epitopes are recognized by individual mabs. This raises the real possibility that some mabs are not derived from a true single cell hybridoma clone. Alternatively, the immunizing antigen may not be pure. Many mabs recognize tissue sections epitopes that are sensitive to chemical fixatives (such as 10% commercial formalin), heat, or exposure to organic solvents (ethanol, toluene, xylene) during tissue processing and embedding in paraffin wax prior to sectioning on a microtome. Thus, the final histologic result achieved using IHC methods may depend not only on antibody purity and specificity, but also on the chemical fixation and tissue processing protocols that were used.

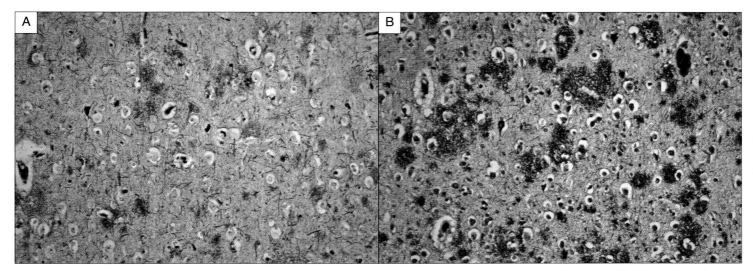

3.9 A: Less intense staining of Alzheimer senile plaques (SP) by the modified Bielschowsky (mBT; 20% silver nitrate) method, compared to the Hedreen–Bielschowsky (hmBP; 4% cupric nitrate–4% silver nitrate) method (**B**). Neurofibrillary tangles and argyrophilic plaque neurites are best viewed with mBT, while hmBP stained diffuse and neuritic SP are darker and provide enhanced contrast for robust quantitation and detection by image analysis. (Adjacent 6 µm paraffin section, ×10 objective.)

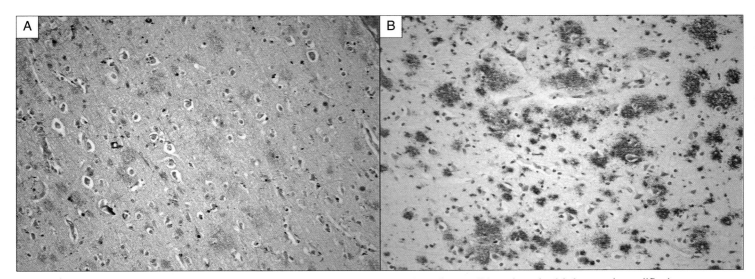

3.10 Alzheimer senile plaque detection is often less robust comparing the traditional and widely used modified Bielschowsky silver method (**A**) with the more modern beta-amyloid immunohistochemical technique employing a brown diaminobenzidine substrate (**B**) on near-serial 6 µm paraffin sections (×10 objective).

There are numerous examples from the AD field where the immunogen was 'purified tangles', yet some resulting antibodies when applied to AD brain tissue labeled SPs instead of NFTs (Masters *et al.*, 1985; Schmidt *et al.*, 1997)! Another example where disparate staining results can arise during immunostaining is the antibody Alz-50 (Ksiezak-Reding *et al.*, 1988) directed near the N-terminus of tau. The 441 amino acid tau molecule becomes truncated by proteolysis as AD progresses. Hippocampal CA1, entorhinal cortex and cortical areas of neuron loss and intense tangle formation ultimately result in conversion of some intraneuronal NFTs to the extracellular form (Augustinack *et al.*, 2001; Vickers *et al.*, 2003). Alz-50 IHC may show reduced labeling of tangles as a result. Such 'immunonegative' tangles, which nevertheless exist but can't be 'seen' by particular antibodies, may produce spuriously low quantitative counts when assessed by image analysis or stereologic techniques, for example.

None of the many steps in IHC staining methods have yet been standardized. This applies to type and times of fixation, embedding parameters including the effects of use of different 'paraffin' preparations that differ in composition (many contain 'plasticizers' and proprietary [unnamed] components, for example), application of antigen 'rescue' or 'unmasking' techniques, and the use of standardized antibodies or working dilutions, buffers, and substrates to name but some of the nonstandardized steps common to all immunostaining procedures. A working committee of European Neuropathologists is working on standardizing neuropathologic IHC methodology (Dennis Dickson, AANP 6/23/04, comment to Li *et al.*, 2004 [agonal factors on human CNS biochemistry]).

Gallyas silver method

This now widely used silver method uses a different underlying principle than the Bielschowsky methods. The Washington University ADRC has adapted the Gallyas method of Braak and Braak (1991b) to 6 μm paraffin sections in order to demonstrate a range of pathologic lesions. The Gallyas method is especially useful for visualizing extracellular and neuronal tangles, argyrophilic grain pathology, tau-positive neuritic changes, and glioneuronal inclusions in FTD tauopathic disorders, in displaying glial cell inclusions (GCI) to define multiple system atrophy (MSA) cases, and as another method to see CAA in paraffin sections (**3.11**). This list of Gallyas silver-positive lesions is not meant to be exhaustive.

IHC methods

Some caveats that have been expressed about interpreting results of IHC methodology in diagnosing dementing disorders have been covered in the preceding section. These limitations should be considered when choosing a particular antibody to use for diagnostic purposes. Unlike many clinical laboratory procedures, IHC methods with rare exceptions (ERB and HER-1 for breast cancer, for example) have not been subject to regulation or accreditation programs. Hospital-based diagnostic pathology laboratories are stringently regulated in the US; however, many IHC techniques are carried out in unregulated research laboratories.

The following IHC methods identify the major diagnostic cellular features for five major groups of neurodegenerative disorders: (1) AD – a-beta and tau; (2) Lewy disorders including MSA with GCI – alpha-synucleinopathies; (3) FTD disorders – tau, ubiquitin; (4) MND – alpha-synuclein, tau, ubiquitin; (5) vascular disease, cerebral angiopathy – a-beta amyloid; (6) disorders with gliosis – glial fibrillary acidic protein (GFAP); and (7) cerebral synapses – synaptophysin. *Box 3.2* describes the IHC markers for neurodegenerative diseases.

Beta amyloid (a-beta) IHC

Liberation of a 4 kd protein from insoluble brain amyloid fibrils was due to the use of formic acid (Klunk *et al.*, 1994). Selkoe *et al.* (1986) soon showed that '4 kd peptide' was the principle component of AD plaques. 4 kd was equivalent to the 40–43 amino acid beta amyloid protein discovered by Glenner and Wong (1984). A number of well characterized mabs directed at full length, 1–40 and 1–42 a-beta protein are now commercially available for use on paraffin sections of formalin fixed (PSFF) brains.

4G8 is a widely used mab that robustly immunostains full length a-beta in PSFF (Kraszpulski *et al.*, 1998). The 6F/3D a-beta clone also produced similar results. 'End specific' mabs that selectively recognized a-beta 1–40 and a-beta 1–42 in PSFF are also available from multiple commercial sources. Representative results using 10D5 (a gift of Dale Schenk at Elan Pharmaceuticals) and 4G8 a-beta mabs on normal and AD brains are shown in **3.12**.

3.11 A–D: Gallyas silver method applied to 6 μm paraffin human brain sections.
A: Demonstration of three major Alzheimer lesions: neuritic senile plaques (arrow), neurofibrillary tangles (short arrow), and neuropil threads (arrowhead) (×20 objective).
B: Two leptomeningeal microaneurysms (Gallyas-negative) surrounded by Gallyas-positive beta amyloid laden arteries (×10 objective).

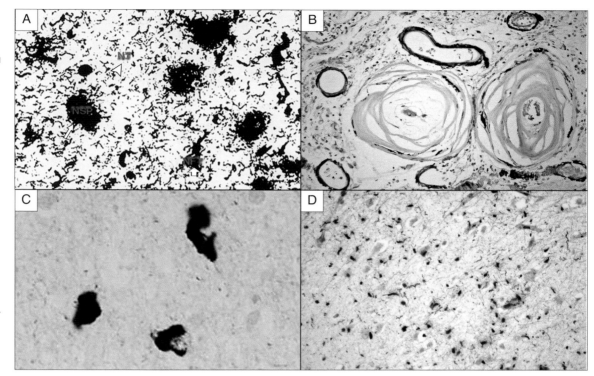

C: Defining glial cell inclusions (GCI) in a case of multiple system atrophy (×40 objective). GCI are also labeled with alpha-synuclein antibodies (not shown here).
D: Argyrophilic grains of Braak in the entorhinal cortex of a patient with argyrophilic grain disease (×20 objective).

Box 3.2 Selected immunohistochemical markers for common lesions in neurodegenerative disease brains

- IL1-A (interleukin-1 alpha), LN-3 for activated microglia
- GFAP (glial fibrillary acidic protein) for normal and gliotic astrocytes
- Synaptophysin, synapsin, SNAP-25, alpha-synuclein for synapses
- Neuronal markers: Neu-N, ChAT (choline acetyltransferase) for cholinergic neurons, DBH (dopamine beta-hydroxylase) for dopaminergic neurons, TH (tyrosine hydroxylase) for noradrenergic neurons; Note: NSE (neuron specific enolase) is not entirely specific for neurons
- Dendritic spine markers: drebrin (Shim & Lubec, 2002)
- Myelin markers: MBP (myelin basic protein), ubiquitin (granular degeneration of aging)
- Alpha-synuclein for Lewy body and neurite pathology, GCI (glial cell inclusions) in multiple system atrophy, corpora amylacea
- Beta amyloid: Alzheimer senile plaques, cerebral amyloid angiopathy
- Hyperphosphorylated tau for Alzheimer neurofibrillary tangles and neuropil threads, Pick body inclusions, astrocytic plaques in corticobasal ganglionic degeneration, tufted astrocytes in progressive supranuclear palsy, argyrophilic grains of Braak in argyrophilic grain disease, and distinctive glial and neuronal inclusions in various tauopathies
- Alpha-internexin and neurofilament subunits for pathological neurofilament inclusions
- Ubiquitin for corpora amylacea, Lewy bodies and neurites, dentate fascia inclusions in frontotemporal dementia with motor neuron diseases, and dementia lacking distinctive histopathology
- Prion antibodies for transmissible spongiform encephalopathies (spontaneous and variant Creutzfeldt–Jakob disease), bovine spongiform encephalopathy, fatal familial insomnia, Gerstmann–Sträussler–Scheinker disease

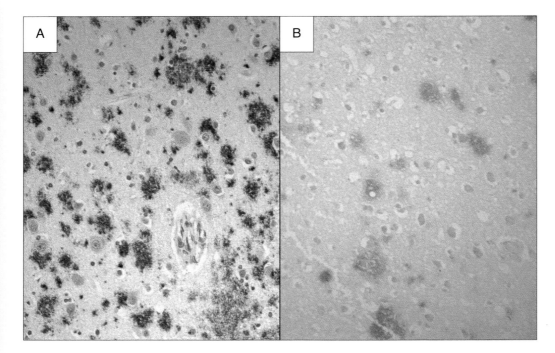

3.12 Near-serial neocortical sections from an Alzheimer case reveal differences in beta-amyloid labeling by specific monoclonal antibody reagents using the brown diaminobenzamidine (DAB) substrate (**A**; 10D5, a gift from Athena/Elan and Dale Schenk) compared to red alkaline phosphatase (**B**; 4G8). Often the two substrates and antibodies provide comparable a-beta immunostaining results. 4G8 'sees' granular peri-Purkinje neuronal cerebellar deposits that are absent using 10D5 (×10 objective).

Tau IHC

Peter Davies and colleagues (Ksiezak-Reding *et al.*, 1988; Rye *et al.*, 1993) described an antibody (Alz-50) directed to the A68 antigen that was elevated in AD brains. Later, A68 was found (probably) to be a form of altered tau protein. Antibodies to certain hyperphosphorylated forms of tau protein that were specific for paired helical filament (PHF) component in AD neurofibrillary lesions were shown not to stain normal brain tau (Rye *et al.*, 1993). Today, 'PHFtau' antibodies directed to known phosphorylated sites on tau are widely used to visualize AD tangles, neuropil threads (NTs), and plaques, dystrophic neurites in AD brains, tau lesions in FTD tauopathies, and tangles that occur, for example, in PSP, postencephalitic parkinsonism, boxers' brains, and entorhinal cortex in normal aging.

The monoclonal antibody PHF-1 labels phosphorylated serines at positions 396 and 404 of tau (Greenberg *et al.*, 1992). This mab robustly immunostains PHFtau but not normal tau in paraffin sections of formalin fixed mammalian brain tissue. Mab AT8 produces very similar results (Kitamura *et al.*, 2005) (**3.13**). It, too, is directed at specific phosphorylation sites at positions serine 202 and threonine 205 of the tau molecule.

Combined IHC for a-beta and tau

At the author's ADRC a dual IHC method is used that combines a-beta 4G8 mab IHC with either PHF-1 or AT8 mab IHC. As shown in figure **3.14**, use of an alkaline phosphatase red substrate for a-beta and a blue-black substrate for PHFtau provides striking delineation of tau-positive neuritic plaques and tau-negative diffuse and preamyloid plaques simultaneously with a-beta immunoreactivity. At the same time, tau-positive NFTs and NTs display the full range of AD neurofibrillary pathology.

Alpha synuclein IHC

A major breakthrough in understanding the pathogenesis of Lewy body disorders (PD, DLB) was the recognition that the presynaptic protein alpha-synuclein became translocated in PD and DLB to form insoluble aggregates in the cytoplasm (classic and cortical Lewy bodies) as well as 'Lewy neurites' (LNs). LNs are akin to tau-positive NTs in AD. In the so-called CA2/3 sector of the hippocampus, which studies indicate often occupies the CA2/1 junctional area, cases of combined AD and PD/DLB may show florid accumulation of PHFtau and alpha-synuclein-positive immunoreactive neurites (**3.15**). It has not been well

3.13 An example of staining patterns of two among many robust hyperphosphorylated tau antibodies that are available to label cytoskeletal abnormalities in neurodegenerative disorders. **A**: Robust PHF-1 (a generous gift of Dr Peter Davies) immunostaining of hippocampal CA1 pathologic tangles and neuropil threads in advanced AD (×10). **B**: Equally robust labeling of a dense meshwork of neuropil threads, senile plaques, and neurofibrillary tangles by commercial tau antibody AT8 in the cerebral cortex of another advanced AD patient (×10 objective hematoxylin counterstain with DAB brown substrate). (Compare to **3.11**.)

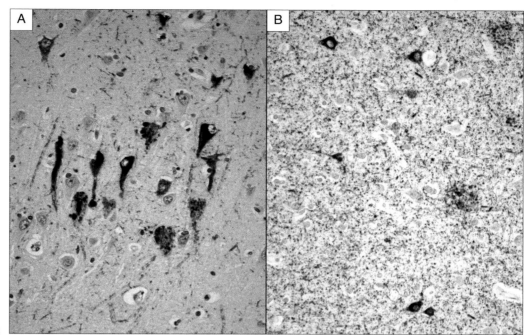

3.14 Combining a-beta (antibody 4G8 or 10D5, red alkaline phosphate substrate) with tau (antibodies PHF- or AT8, true blue substrate) has proven very useful to discriminate conclusively tau-negative (red only, preamyloid and diffuse) and tau-positive (red with black, neuritic) senile plaques (one is shown at 3 o'clock), while simultaneously labeling black neurofibrillary tangles (at 9 o'clock position), neuropil threads (shown) and vascular beta amyloid (not illustrated) (×20 objective, 6 μm paraffin brain section).

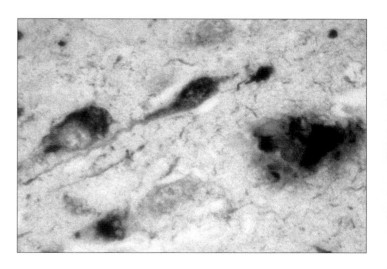

3.15 Antibody to the presynaptic protein alpha-synuclein (Zymed LB-509 monoclonal antibody shown here) is the current method of choice for demonstrating Lewy pathology in dementia with Lewy bodies. A cortical Lewy body, a type of neuronal cytoplasmic inclusion, is shown at upper left, while a huge Lewy 'mega-neurite' is shown at lower right. Finer linear Lewy neurites are scattered through the field. Round punctate tiny objects are antibody labeled individual synapses (×40 objective).

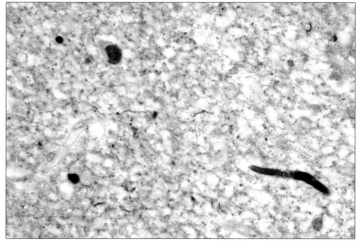

established whether or not individual neuritic processes are co-labeled by both antibodies or whether co-mingled tau- and alpha synuclein-positive neuritic elements are observed.

Ubiquitin IHC

Proteins destined for cellular elimination are targeted to the 26S cytoplasmic proteosome by being 'tagged' by ubiquitin. There is additional recent evidence that alpha-synuclein and ubiquitin are both integral components of Lewy bodies (Snyder and Wolozin, 2004). Ubiquitin labels Lewy bodies, corpora amylacea (CA), some AD plaque and neuropil neurites, subsets of NFTs in AD brains, and white matter 'granular degeneration', a near universal accompaniment of human aging (**3.16**) (also see Chapter 4) (Wang *et al.*, 2004). Many polyclonal and monoclonal antibodies to

ubiquitin are commercially available. The author uses a polyclonal antibody from East Acres to achieve robust staining using PSFF. More recently, a mouse monoclonal antiubiquitin antibody has proven to be even more sensitive for detecting cytoplasmic and nuclear inclusions in cases of FTD–MND (**3.16**).

GFAP IHC

GFAP is the main component of one class of intermediate filament proteins that are found in astrocytic glial cells (Roelofs *et al.*, 2005). Pathologists use GFAP IHC to define 'gliosis'. This term refers to abnormal hypertrophy and hyperplasia of astrocytes in various pathologic disorders that range from normal aging, to brain infarction, to areas of neuron loss in AD and FTD (**3.17**).

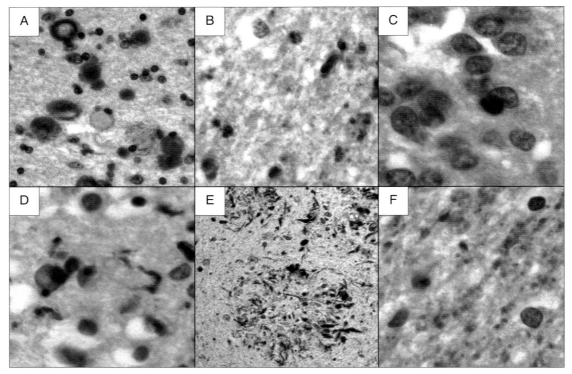

3.16 A–F: East Acres polyclonal ubiquitin antiserum labeling. **A**: Strongly immunolabeled corpora amylacea (×20 objective). **B**: Rounded profiles, probably cross-sectioned dendrites, of unknown diagnostic significance, in the subiculum (×40 objective). **C**: Ubiquinated inclusions in dentate fascia neurons (×40 objective). **D**: Irregular curly ubiquinated neurites in neocortex of a frontotemporal dementia case (×40 objective). **E**: Strong ubiquitin labeling of neuritic plaque neurites in hippocampal area CA4 of an Alzheimer patient (×20 objective). **F**: Aging related, ubiquitin-positive, granular degeneration of the white matter (×40 objective).

Synaptophysin IHC

Human brain synapses contain multiple marker proteins (Lippa *et al.*, 1992) that may be used to identify them in biochemical assays (dot and Western blotting) as well as by IHC on tissue sections (**3.18**) (Reddy *et al.*, 2005). Synapse protein quantification may be successfully achieved using optical density measurements of the IHC reaction product (Lippa *et al.*, 1992) or by counting the total number of synapses in a brain reference volume using unbiased stereology at the light (Calhoun *et al.*, 1996; DW McKeel, Jr and NS Havlioglu, unpublished data on 20 subjects CDR 0–3) or the ultrastructural (electron microscopic) level (DeKosky *et al.*, 1996). In the author's experience, excellent robust synaptophysin IHC results may be obtained on formalin-fixed paraffin-embedded (FFPE) brain sections up to 48 hours postmortem. A minority of brains (~20%) for unknown reasons fail to stain robustly enough with synaptophysin antibodies to perform stereologic analysis (NS Havlioglu and DW McKeel, Jr, unpublished data).

Synaptophysin immunoreactivity was decreased significantly in both AD prefrontal cortex (Masliah *et al.*, 2001) and in terminal fields of the perforant pathway located in the molecular layer of the hippocampal dentate fascia (Morys *et al.*, 1994; NS Havlioglu and DW McKeel, Jr, unpublished data) in brains from patients with very mild (CDR 0.5) AD. The latter study revealed that synaptophysin immunoreactivity declined throughout the CDR with a Pearson correlation between last CDR and total synapse number in the entire left hippocampus of r = 0.85. Unbiased sampling and stereology methodology thus produced the highest positive correlation observed between AD dementia severity (CDR assessment) and an established neuropathology biomarker of disease.

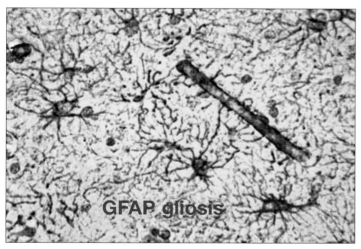

3.17 Astrocytic hypertrophy and hyperplasia, gliosis, is a fundamental pathologic process in many neuro-degenerative disorders. Antibodies to glial fibrillary acid protein, a class of astrocytic intermediate filaments, is extensively used to reveal pathologic gliosis in human neuropathology. (DAB substrate, 6 µm paraffin section, ×20 objective.)

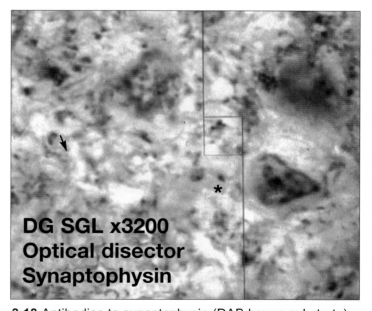

3.18 Antibodies to synaptophysin (DAB brown substrate) are often used to label and quantify synapses as shown here in the hippocampal dentate fascia. Clusters and individual synapses may be seen within the superimposed frame of the optical disector (asterisk: out of frame in focus synapse, arrow: out of frame, out of focus plane synapse), when viewed at ×3200 final magnification with the PC-based Stereologer™ image analysis and stereology system. The cellular nuclei have been counterstained with hematoxylin (×100 oil immersion). (DG, dentate gyrus; SGL supragranular layer.)

Newer diagnostic methods for dementing disorders

Newer diagnostic methods have been developed that provide major insights into key mechanisms of disease that determine cognitive impairment and dementia across the spectrum of related disorders. Some of them are described in the following sections.

Tissue microarrays

Tissue microarrays (Sjobeck *et al.*, 2003; Simon *et al.*, 2005), small cores of paraffin embedded formalin-fixed archival brain tissue, are re-embedded in new paraffin blocks in a 'row and column matrix' of similar sized tissue cores on a regular 1 × 3 inch glass slide (**3.19**). Depending on the diameter of each core (usually 0.6–3 mm), densities as high as 50–100 cores per slide can be constructed. In this manner, new antibodies can be screened, or series of similar cases can be assessed for individual case differences to, for example, a single standard antibody (**3.20**).

Laser capture tissue microdissection and biochemical microanalysis

Laser and microscope-based instrumentation is now available so that single cells or lesions, such as individual Alzheimer SPs, may be isolated with the laser from a fixed histologic section, affixed onto film, and carried through staining solutions or pooled for biochemical microanalysis. Nucleic acid concentrations including mRNA may be determined. This technology is finding wide application in neurodegenerative disease research (Hyman *et al.*, 2005; Standaert, 2005).

Multiphoton brain tissue microscopy

Single, dual, triple, or even four-photon microscopic methods are available to visualize structures located several hundred microns below the brain surface in living animals (Denk *et al.*, 1994). Typical applications involve introduction of tracers directly onto the brain surface or intravenously. For example, a brain soluble marker, such as the fluorescent dye thioflavine S, can gain entry into the

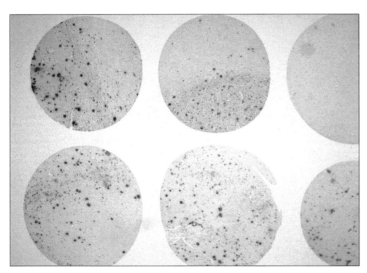

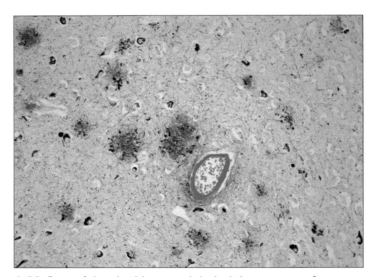

3.19 Six cerebral cortex cores of a neurodegenerative disorders tissue microarray are shown after staining with anti-4G8 (amyloid beta) and AT8 tau antibody dual label immunohistochemistry (please refer to **3.14**). Blank microarray slide courtesy of Dr Irina Alafuzoff as part of a NACC methodological collaborative study between European and US Alzheimer Disease Center neuropathology laboratories. Note absence of both a-beta and tau labeling in the section at far upper right, and variable amounts of amyloid (red) and tau (black) among the other brain tissue cores (×1 objective). (Compare with figure **3.20**.)

3.20 One of the dual immunolabeled tissue cores from **3.19** is shown at higher magnification to display quality of staining. The result is in every way comparable to larger sections that have been individually processed and stained. Neuritic senile plaques, neurofibrillary tangles, neuropil threads, and parenchymal vascular amyloid deposition are clearly revealed in the small tissue core sample (×10 objective). (Compare with figure **3.19**.)

brain through a thin or open window in the skull (D'Amore et al., 2003). The dye infiltrates the brain and rapidly binds to senile plaques which fluoresce. By carefully marking the 3-dimensional spatial location of a particular plaque, serial observations are possible over time as to whether the plaque grows in size, maintains a stable size, or diminishes in size and disappears. Examples of all three types have been observed in mouse models of AD (Christie et al., 2001).

Determination of beta-amyloid load or burden

Image analysis and stereologic methods may be used to quantify the fractional area occupied by beta-amyloid protein in histologic slides of brain neocortex. This approach obviates the tedious task of counting thousands of individual Alzheimer senile plaques in a single tissue section. This measure has been referred to as the 'amyloid burden' or the 'amyloid load' (Hyman et al., 1993; Leverenz et al., 1998) (**3.21**).

New combinatorial or hybrid methods to visualize AD lesions

Rapid advances in biomedical engineering, in the physical and chemical sciences, and in molecular biology, have led to powerful methods to gain insights into mechanisms of neurodegenerative diseases, including EM and stereology (Dunckley et al., 2006), comparing IHC with quantitative AD marker biochemistry (Feany & Dickson, 1996; Jackson and Lowe, 1996), and multiphoton microscopy of fluorescent oxidation products that localize in senile plaques (McLellan et al., 2003). The development of in vivo radiochemical probes that bind directly to senile plaques allowing them to be visualized in living patients by positive emission tomography (PET) promises to revolutionize AD diagnosis and treatment monitoring (Nordberg, 2004; Verhoeff et al., 2004; Price et al., 2005).

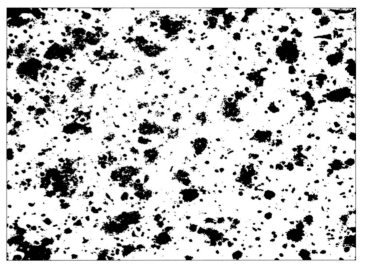

3.21 This color-converted TIFF black and white image of an Alzheimer cerebral cortex 6 μm thick section, which had been stained by an a-beta specific antibody and a link antibody with a red chromogen, was manually thresholded and converted to binary in Adobe *Photoshop CS*. The black senile plaque pixels (44418 pixels) represent 22.16% of the total image area (200720 pixels). The image was captured by an ISI Colorview II™ digital camera at 72 dpi in a 28K × 22K pixel image that then was resized to 6 inches wide by 4.4 inches high at 300 dpi for publication. The section was viewed with a ×10 microscope objective on a Nikon E-800 Eclipse research microscope in the Washington University ADRC Neuropathology Core Laboratory. The basic method is widely used to determine the fractional area ('burden' or 'load') occupied by beta-amyloid protein in the Alzheimer brain. More sophisticated image analysis algorithms are available to generate similar data (Hibbard et al., 1994, 1995, 1997).

References

Akiguchi I, Tomimoto H, Wakita H, *et al.* (2004). Topographical and cytopathological lesion analysis of the white matter in Binswanger's disease brains. *Acta Neuropathol.* **107**:563–570.

Alzheimer A (1907). Über eine eignartiger Erkrankung der Hirnrinde (About a peculiar disease of the cerebral cortex); English translation in *Alz. Dis. Ass. Dis.* **1**:7–8, 1987. *Allgemeine Zeitschrift fur Psychiatrie und Psychisch-Gerichtliche Medizin* **64**:146–148.

Augustinack JC, Schneider A, Mandelkow EM, *et al.* (2002). Specific tau phosphorylation sites correlate with severity of neuronal cytopathology in Alzheimer's disease. *Acta Neuropathol.* **103**:26–35.

Bellomo G, Santambrogio L, Fiacconi M, *et al.* (1991). Plasma profiles of adrenocorticotropic hormone, cortisol, growth hormone, and prolactin in patients with untreated Parkinson's disease. *J. Neurol.* **238**:19–22.

Berg L, McKeel DW, Jr., Miller JP, *et al.* (1998). Clinicopathologic studies in cognitively healthy aging and Alzheimer disease: relation of histologic markers to dementia severity, age, sex, and apolipoprotein E genotype. *Arch. Neurol.* **55**:326–335.

Bertram L, Tanzi RE (2004). The current status of Alzheimer's disease genetics: what do we tell the patients? [Review] [83 refs] *Pharmacol. Res.* **50**:385–396.

Blackwell AD, Sahakian BJ, Vesey R, *et al.* (2004). Detecting dementia: novel neuropsychological markers of preclinical Alzheimer's disease. *Dementia & Geriatric Cognitive Dis.* **17**:42–48.

Braak H, Braak E (1991a). The neuropathologic stageing of Alzheimer-related changes. *Acta Neuropathol* (Berlin) **82**:239–259.

Braak H, Braak E (1991b). Demonstration of amyloid deposits and neurofibrillary changes in whole brain sections. *Brain Pathol.* **1**:213–216.

Brendza RP, O'Brien C, Simmons K, *et al.* (2003). PDAPP YFP double transgenic mice: a tool to study amyloid-beta associated changes in axonal, dendritic, and synaptic structures. *J. Comp. Neurol.* **456**:375–383.

Calhoun ME, Jucker M, Martin LJ, *et al.* (1996). Comparative evaluation of synaptophysin-based methods for quantification of synapses. *J. Neurocytol.* **25**:821–828.

Christie RH, Bacskai BJ, Zipfel WR, *et al.* (2001). Growth arrest of individual senile plaques in a model of Alzheimer's disease observed by *in vivo* multiphoton microscopy. *J. Neurosci.* **21**:858–864.

Crystal H, Dickson D, Fuld P, *et al.* (1988). Clinico-pathologic studies in dementia. Nondemented subjects with pathologically confirmed Alzheimer's disease. *Neurology* **38**:1682–1687.

Cullen KM, Halliday GM, Cartwright H, *et al.* (1996). Improved selectivity and sensitivity in the visualization of neurofibrillary tangles, plaques and neuropil threads. *Neurodegeneration* **5**:177–187.

D'Amore JD, Kajdasz ST, McLellan ME, *et al.* (2003). *In vivo* multiphoton imaging of a transgenic mouse model of Alzheimer disease reveals marked thioflavine-S-associated alterations in neurite trajectories. *J. Neuropathol. Exp. Neurol.* **62**:137–145.

de Carvalho M (2001). Pathophysiological significance of fasciculations in the early diagnosis of ALS. *Amyotrophic Lateral Sclerosis & Other Motor Neuron Disorders* Suppl **1**:S43–S46.

DeKosky ST, Scheff SW, Styren SD (1996). Structural correlates of cognition in dementia: quantification and assessment of synapse change. [Review] [32 refs] *Neurodegeneration* **5**:417–421.

Denk W, Delaney KR, Gelperin A, *et al.* (1994). Anatomical and functional imaging of neurons using 2-photon laser scanning microscopy. [Review] [35 refs] *J. Neurosci. Meth.* **54**:151–162.

Desai AK, Grossberg GT (2005). Diagnosis and treatment of Alzheimer's disease. *Neurology* **64**(12 Suppl 3):S34–S39.

Delacourte A, Defossez A, Persuy P, *et al.* (1987). Observation of morphological relationships between angiopathic blood vessels and degenerative neurites in Alzheimer's disease. *Virchows Archiv – A, Pathological Anatomy & Histopathology* **411**:199–204.

Dickson DW (2003). *Neurodegeneration: The Molecular Pathology of Dementia and Movement Disorders.* ISN Neuropath. Press, Basel.

Dunckley T, Beach TG, Ramsey K, *et al.* (2006). Gene expression correlates of neurofibrillary tangles in Alzheimer's disease. *Neurobiol. Aging* **27**:1359–1371.

Esiri MM, Hyman BT, Beyreuther K, *et al.* (1997). Ageing and dementia. In: *Greenfield's Neuropathology* (6th edn.). DI Graham, PL Lantos (eds.). Arnold, London, pp. 153–234.

Esiri MM, Lee V-MY, Trojanowski JQ (ed.) (2004). *The Neuropathology of Dementia.* Cambridge University Press, Cambridge.

Feany MB, Dickson DW (1996). Neurodegenerative disorders with extensive tau pathology: a comparative study and review. [Review] [93 refs] *Ann. Neurol.* **40**:139–148.

Flynn MD, Cundy TF, Watkins PJ (1988). Antepartum pituitary necrosis in diabetes mellitus. [Review] [10 refs] *Diabetic Med.* **5**:295–297.

Forman MS, Lee VM, Trojanowski JQ (2005a). Nosology of Parkinson's disease: looking for the way out of a quagmire. [Review] [26 refs] *Neuron* **47**:479–482.

Forman MS, Mackenzie IR, Markesbery WR, *et al.* (2005b). Novel ubiquitin brain pathology in frontotemporal dementia with inclusion body myopathy and Paget's disease. (abstract 12) Am. Assoc. Neuropathol. *J. Neuropathol. Exp. Neurol.* **64**:433.

Fowler MR, McKeel DW Jr (1979a). Human adenohypophyseal quantitative histochemical cell classification. I. Morphologic criteria and cell type distribution. *Arch. Pathol. Lab. Med.* **103**:613–620.

Fowler MR, McKeel DW Jr (1979b). Human adenohypophyseal quantitative histochemical cell classification. II. Evaluation of the effects of two fixatives and postmortem interval. *Arch. Pathol. Lab. Med.* **103**:621–623.

Games D, Adams D, Allesandrini R, *et al.* (1991). Alzheimer-type neuropathology in transgenic mice overexpressing V717F beta-amyloid precursor protein. *Nature* **349**:704–706.

Giannakopoulos P, Hof PR, Kovari E, *et al.* (1996). Distinct patterns of neuronal loss and Alzheimer's disease lesion distribution in elderly individuals older than 90 years. *J. Neuropathol. Exp. Neurol.* **55**:1210–1220.

Glenner GG, Wong CW (1984). Alzheimer's disease: initial report of the purification and characterization of a novel cerebrovascular amyloid protein. *Biochem. Biophys. Res. Comm.* **120**:885–890.

Goldman WP, Storandt M, Miller JP, *et al.* (2001). Mild cognitive impairment represents early-stage Alzheimer's disease. *Arch. Neurol.* **58**:397–405.

Greenberg SG, Davies P, Schein JD, *et al.* (1992). Hydrofluoric acid-treated tau PHF proteins display the same biochemical properties as normal tau. *J. Biol. Chem.* **267**:564–569.

Grundman M, Petersen RC, Ferris SH, *et al.* (2004). Alzheimer's Disease Cooperative Study. Mild cognitive impairment can be distinguished from Alzheimer disease and normal aging for clinical trials. *Arch. Neurol.* **61**:59–66.

Hibbard LS, McKeel DW Jr, Arnicar-Sulze TL, *et al.* (1994). Automated detection and morphological analysis of senile plaques in SDAT. *J. Neurosci. Meth.* **52**:175–189.

Hibbard LS, McKeel DW Jr (1995). Multiscale detection and analysis of senile plaques of Alzheimer's disease. *IEEE Transactions on Pattern Analysis and Machine Intelligence* **42**:1218–1225.

Hibbard LS, McKeel DW Jr (1997). Automated identification and quantitative morphometry of the senile plaques of Alzheimer's disease. *Analytical Quant. Cytol. Histol.* **19**:123–138.

Holton JL, Révész T, Crooks R, *et al.* (2001). Evidence for pathological involvement of the spinal cord in motor neuron disease-inclusion dementia. *Acta Neuropathol.* **103**:221–227.

Horvath E, Kovacs K, Scheithauer BW (1999). Pituitary hyperplasia. [Review] [60 refs] *Pituitary* **1**:169–179.

Hughes CP, Berg L, Danziger WL, *et al.* (1982). A new clinical scale for the staging of dementia. *Br. J. Psych.* **140**:566–572.

Hyman BT, Augustinack JC, Ingelsson M (2005). Transcriptional and conformational changes of the tau molecule in Alzheimer's disease. [Review] [73 refs] *Biochim. Biophys. Acta* **1739**:150–157.

Hyman BT, Marzloff K, Arriagada PV (1993). The lack of accumulation of senile plaques or amyloid burden in Alzheimer's disease suggests a dynamic balance between amyloid deposition and resolution. *J. Neuropathol. Exp. Neurol.* **52**:594–600.

Jackson M, Lowe J (1996). The new neuropathology of degenerative frontotemporal dementias. [Review] [38 refs] *Acta Neuropathol.* **91**:127–134.

Josephson SA, Schmidt RE, Millsap P, *et al.* (2001). Autosomal dominant Kufs' disease: a cause of early onset dementia. *J. Neurol. Sci.* **188**:51–60.

Kato S, Hirano A, Llena JF (1992). Immuno-histochemical, ultrastructural, and immunoelectron microscopic studies of spinal cord neurofibrillary tangles in progressive supranuclear palsy. *Neuropathol. Appl. Neurobiol.* **18**:531–538.

Kanda T, Tsukagoshi H, Oda M, *et al.* (1996). Changes of unmyelinated nerve fibers in sural nerve in amyotrophic lateral sclerosis, Parkinson's disease, and multiple system atrophy. *Acta Neuropathol.* **91**:145–154.

Katzman R, Terry R, De Teresa R, *et al.* (1988). Clinical, pathological, and neurochemical changes in dementia: a subgroup with preserved mental status and numerous neocortical plaques. *Ann. Neurol.* **23**:138–144.

Kingsbury AE, Foster OJ, Nisbet AP, *et al.* (1995). Tissue pH as an indicator of mRNA preservation in human postmortem brain. *Brain Res. Mol. Brain Res.* **28**:311–318.

Kirshner HS (2005). Mild cognitive impairment: to treat or not to treat. *Curr. Neurol. Neurosci. Rep.* **5**:455–457.

Kitamura T, Sugimori K, Sudo S, *et al.* (2005). Relationship between microtubule-binding repeats and morphology of neurofibrillary tangle in Alzheimer's disease. *Acta Neurol. Scand.* **112**:327–334.

Khachaturian ZS (1985). Diagnosis of Alzheimer's disease. *Arch. Neurol.* **42**:1097–1105.

Klunk WE, Xu CJ, Pettegrew JW (1994). NMR identification of the formic acid-modified residue in Alzheimer's amyloid protein. *J. Neurochem.* **62**:349–354.

Klüver and Barrera (1953). A method for the combined staining of cells and fibers in the central nervous system. *J. Neuropath. Exp. Neurol.* **12**:400–403.

Kraszpulski M, Soininen H, Riekkinen P Sr, *et al.* (1998). Pitfalls in the quantitative estimation of beta-amyloid immunoreactivity in human brain tissue. *Histochem. Cell Biol.* **110**:439–445.

Ksiezak-Reding H, Davies P, Yen SH (1988). Alz-50, a monoclonal antibody to Alzheimer's disease antigen, cross-reacts with tau proteins from bovine and normal human brain. *J. Biol. Chem.* **263**:7943–7947.

Leverenz JB, Raskind MA (1998). Early amyloid deposition in the medial temporal lobe of young Down syndrome patients: a regional quantitative analysis. *Exp. Neurol.* **150**:296–304.

Li JZ, Vawter MP, Walsh DM, *et al.* (2004). Systematic changes in gene expression in postmortem human brains associated with tissue pH and terminal medical conditions. *Human Mol. Genet.* **13**:609–616.

Lippa CF, Hamos JE, Pulaski-Salo D, *et al.* (1992). Alzheimer's disease and aging: effects on perforant pathway perikarya and synapses. *Neurobiol. Aging* **13**:405–411.

Lowe J (1998). Establishing a neuropathological diagnosis in degenerative dementias. *Brain Pathol.* **8**:403–406.

Luna L (1968). *Manual of Histologic Staining Methods of the AFIP* (3rd edn.) McGraw-Hill Book Co., New York, pp. 203–204.

Luna L (1968). Schiff Reagent for the PAS (periodic acid-Schiff) stain: 21b. In: *Manual of Histologic Staining Methods of the AFIP* (3rd edn.) McGraw-Hill Book Co., New York, p. 159.

Luna-Munoz J, Garcia-Sierra F, Falcon V, *et al.* (2005). Regional conformational change involving phosphorylation of tau protein at the Thr231, precedes the structural change detected by Alz-50 antibody in Alzheimer's disease. *J. Alz. Dis.* **8**:29–41.

Markesbery WR (1998). *Neuropathology of Dementing Disorders*. Edward Arnold (Publishers) Limited, London. ISBN 0-340-59037-8; EAN: 9780340590379, pp. 404.

Masliah E, Mallory M, Alford M, *et al.* (2001). Altered expression of synaptic proteins occurs early during progression of Alzheimer's disease. *Neurology* **56**:127–129.

Masters CL, Multhaup G, Simms G, *et al.* (1985). Neuronal origin of a cerebral amyloid: neurofibrillary tangles of Alzheimer's disease contain the same protein as the amyloid of plaque cores and blood vessels. *EMBO J.* **4**:2757–2763.

McKeel DW Jr, Ball MJ, Price JL, *et al.* (1993). Interlaboratory histopathologic assessment of Alzheimer neuropathology: different methodologies yield comparable diagnostic results. *Alz. Dis. Assoc. Dis.* **7**:136–151.

McKeel DW Jr, Price JL, Miller, JP, *et al.* (2004). Neuropathologic criteria for diagnosing Alzheimer disease in persons with pure dementia of Alzheimer type. *J. Neuropathol. Exp. Neurol.* **63**:1028–1037.

McLellan ME, Kajdasz ST, Hyman BT, *et al.* (2003). *In vivo* imaging of reactive oxygen species specifically associated with thioflavine S-positive amyloid plaques by multiphoton microscopy. *J. Neurosci.* **23**:2212–2217.

Mirra SS, Gearing M, McKeel DW Jr, *et al.* (1994) Interlaboratory comparison of neuropathologic assessments in Alzheimer's disease: a study of the Consortium to Establish a Registry for Alzheimer's disease (CERAD). *J. Neuropathol. Exp. Neurol.* **53**:303–315.

Mirra SS, Heyman A, McKeel D Jr, *et al.* (1991). The Consortium to Establish a Registry for Alzheimer's Disease (CERAD). Part II. Standardization of the neuropathologic assessment of Alzheimer's disease. *Neurology* **41**:479–486.

Morihara T, Kudo T, Ikura Y, *et al.* (1998). Increased tau protein level in postmortem cerebrospinal fluid. *Psych. Clin. Neurosci.* **52**:107–110.

Morris JC (1993). The Clinical Dementia Rating (CDR): current version and scoring rules.[see comment]. *Neurology* **43**:2412–2414.

Morris JC, Price JL (2001). Pathologic correlates of nondemented aging, mild cognitive impairment, and early-stage Alzheimer's disease. [Review] [110 refs] *J. Mol. Neurosci.* **17**:101–118.

Morris JC, Storandt M, McKeel DW Jr, *et al.* (1996). Cerebral amyloid deposition and diffuse plaques in 'normal' aging: evidence for presymptomatic and very mild Alzheimer's disease. *Neurology* **46**:707–719.

Morys J, Sadowski M, Barcikowska M, *et al.* (1994). The second layer neurones of the entorhinal cortex and the perforant path in physiological ageing and Alzheimer's disease. *Acta Neurobiol. Exp.* **54**:47–53.

National Institute on Aging, and Reagan Institute Working Group on Diagnostic Criteria for Neuropathological Assessment of Alzheimer's disease (1997). Working Group Consensus Recommendations for the postmortem diagnosis of Alzheimer's disease. *Neurobiol. Aging* **18**(4 Suppl): S1–S2.

Nordberg A (2004). PET imaging of amyloid in Alzheimer's disease. [Review] [80 refs] *Lancet Neurol.* **3**:519–527.

Petersen RC (2004). Mild cognitive impairment as a diagnostic entity. [Review] [50 refs] *J. Int. Med.* **256**:183–194.

Porta EA (2002). Pigments in aging: an overview. [Review] [50 refs] *Ann. N.Y. Acad. Sci.* **959**:57–65.

Price JC, Klunk WE, Lopresti BJ, *et al.* (2005). Kinetic modeling of amyloid binding in humans using PET imaging and Pittsburgh Compound-B. *J. Cereb. Blood Flow Metab.* **25**:1528–1547.

Rademakers R, Cruts M, van Broeckhoven C (2004). The role of tau (MAPT) in frontotemporal dementia and related tauopathies. [Review] [195 refs] *Human Mutation* **24**:277–295.

Reddy PH, Mani G, Park BS, *et al.* (2005). Differential loss of synaptic proteins in Alzheimer's disease: implications for synaptic dysfunction. *J. Alz. Dis.* **7**:103–117; discussion 173–180.

Roelofs RF, Fischer DF, Houtman SH, *et al.* (2005). Adult human subventricular, subgranular, and subpial zones contain astrocytes with a specialized intermediate filament cytoskeleton. *GLIA* **52**:289–300.

Rye DB, Leverenz J, Greenberg SG, *et al.* (1993). The distribution of Alz-50 immunoreactivity in the normal human brain. *Neuroscience* **56**:109–127.

Schmidt ML, Lee VM, Forman M, *et al.* (1997). Monoclonal antibodies to a 100-kD protein reveal abundant A beta-negative plaques throughout gray matter of Alzheimer's disease brains. *Am. J. Pathol.* **151**:69–80.

Selkoe DJ, Abraham CR, Podlisny MB, *et al.* (1986). Isolation of low-molecular weight proteins from amyloid plaque fibers in Alzheimer's disease. *J. Neurochem.* **46**:1820–1824.

Shim KS, Lubec G (2002). Drebrin, a dendritic spine protein, is manifold decreased in brains of patients with Alzheimer's disease and Down syndrome. *Neurosci. Lett.* **324**:209–212.

Simon R, Mirlacher M, Sauter G (2005). Tissue microarrays. *Meth. Molec. Med.* **114**:257–268.

Sjobeck M, Haglund M, Persson A, Sturesson K, Englund E (2003). Brain tissue microarrays in dementia research: white matter microvascular pathology in Alzheimer disease. *Neuropathology* **23**:290–295.

Snyder H, Wolozin B (2004). Pathological proteins in Parkinson's disease: focus on the proteasome. [Review] [179 refs] *J. Mol. Neurosci.* **24**:425–442.

Standaert DG (2005). Applications of laser capture microdissection in the study of neurodegenerative disease. [Review] [10 refs] *Arch. Neurol.* **62**:203–205.

Strozyk D, Blennow K, White LR, *et al.* (2003). CSF Abeta 42 levels correlate with amyloid-neuropathology in a population-based autopsy study. *Neurology* **60**:652–656.

Tagliavini F, Giaccone G, Frangione B, *et al.* (1988). Preamyloid deposits in the cerebral cortex of patients with Alzheimer's disease and nondemented individuals. *Neurosci. Lett.* **93**:191–196.

Troost D, Das PK, van den Oord JJ, *et al.* (1992). Immunohistological alterations in muscle of patients with amyotrophic lateral sclerosis: mononuclear cell phenotypes and expression of MHC products. *Clin. Neuropathol.* **11**:115–120.

Vattemi G, Engel WK, McFerrin J, *et al.* (2003). Cystatin C colocalizes with amyloid-beta and coimmunoprecipitates with amyloid-beta precursor protein in sporadic inclusion-body myositis muscles. *J. Neurochem.* **85**:1539–1546.

Verhoeff NP, Wilson AA, Takeshita S, *et al.* (2004). *In vivo* imaging of Alzheimer disease beta-amyloid with [11C]SB-13 PET. *Am. J. Ger. Psych.* **12**:584–595.

Vickers JC, Tan A, Dickson TC (2003). Direct determination of the proportion of intra- and extracellular neocortical neurofibrillary tangles in Alzheimer's disease. *Brain Res.* **971**:135–137.

Wang DS, Bennett DA, Mufson EJ, *et al.* (2004). Contribution of changes in ubiquitin and myelin basic protein to age-related cognitive decline. *Neurosci. Res.* **48**:93–100.

Watson GS, Craft S (2003). The role of insulin resistance in the pathogenesis of Alzheimer's disease: implications for treatment. [Review] [163 refs] *CNS Drugs* **17**:27–45.

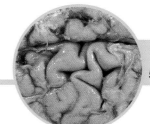

Chapter 4

Neuropathology of healthy brain aging

Introduction

This chapter describes anatomic changes in the brains of persons who are cognitively normal at the time of death and do not have a recognized neurologic illness.

Certain pathologic conditions such as Alzheimer's disease (AD), senile plaques (SPs), and neurofibrillary tangles (NFTs), and the occurrence of 'incidental' brainstem Lewy bodies, are highly age-associated but are not believed to be *caused by* aging *per se*. The implications of such lesions as

possible herald lesions for later development of full-blown disease is discussed in this chapter. Additional discussion may be found in Chapter 5.

Pathologists have long appreciated that many systemic disorders are tightly linked to the aging process. Among these are aortic and major vascular systems atherosclerosis (*Box 4.1*, **4.1**) (Roher *et al.*, 2005) and *in situ* carcinoma of the prostate gland in men. When serial sectioning is applied

Box 4.1 Cerebral atherosclerosis, Alzheimer's disease, and aging

Age is a major risk factor for both cerebral circle of Willis atherosclerosis and Alzheimer senile plaques (SP) (see Chapter 5). The graphs are adapted from a monograph chapter written in 1970 by neuropathologist JAN Corsellis and show the age-related incidences of both types of lesions in an autopsied series of 667 patients from a mental hospital in England. The lesions were graded as less severe (grade 1) and more severe (grades 2 and 3). The incidence of both lesions (y-axis) as percent of cases affected, and severity grades of each, are strikingly related to age at death (x-axis). More modern series based on alpha-beta immunohistochemistry and optimized silver methods for SP would show higher prevalences at the uppermost age ranges. In the authors' experience, more than 90% of persons who die at 90 years or older have some neocortical SP and neurofibrillary tangles in their brains at autopsy. (Adapted from Corsellis, 1970.)

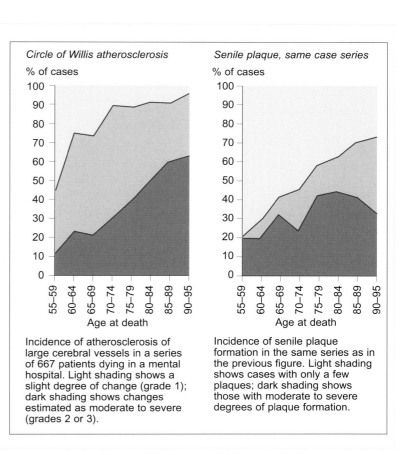

Incidence of atherosclerosis of large cerebral vessels in a series of 667 patients dying in a mental hospital. Light shading shows a slight degree of change (grade 1); dark shading shows changes estimated as moderate to severe (grades 2 or 3).

Incidence of senile plaque formation in the same series as in the previous figure. Light shading shows cases with only a few plaques; dark shading shows those with moderate to severe degrees of plaque formation.

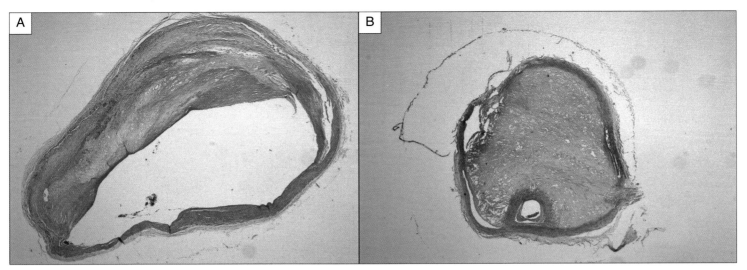

4.1 (A) A cross-section of a major cerebral artery shows approximately 30% occlusion of the lumen by a fibrous atherosclerotic plaque (×1 objective). **(B)** Another circle of Willis major arterial tributary shows almost complete occlusion by a fibrofatty atherosclerotic plaque. The latter lesions with 'critical stenosis' (>75% lumenal narrowing) impair blood flow and cause ischemic strokes if sufficient collateral blood supply is not available to meet tissue needs (×1 objective).

Table 4.1 Features of the aging brain

Anatomic lesions	*Pathologic lesions*
White matter granular degeneration	NFTs in AON, ERC-II, LC, and NBM
Neuronal lipofuscin	Isolated preamyloid and diffuse SP
Corpora amylacea accumulation	CAA
CP calcification	Arterial lipohyalinosis
GFAP mRNA up-regulation	Lacunar infarction
Gracile nucleus neuroaxonal dystrophy	Atherosclerosis of the circle of Willis major arteries
Widened Virchow–Robins spaces reflecting aging-related vascular tortuosity; focal arterial iron/calcium deposition	Hippocampal CA1 GVD (<9% of pyramidal neurons affected)
Localized vertex meningeal fibrosis	Cortical atrophy
Frontal horn rounding (slight)	Ventricular enlargement
Periventricular myelin pallor (MRI and CT 'caps' and 'high signal areas')	Selective neuronal loss (LC, DR, NBM, CA fields of hippocampus, cortex)

to the prostate glands of autopsied 85-years-olds, Franks (1954) reported that minute latent carcinomatous foci were found in prostate glands of all autopsied men aged 90 years or over. This concept of diseases that are *associated with* but are not caused by aging is important. Brains from persons dying after 90 years of age in the authors' experience, even though normal cognition has been established before death, nevertheless have subthreshold AD lesions that may or may not meet established diagnostic criteria for AD. Nevertheless, the *pattern* of such lesions is often so typical of AD lesion location and distribution as to suggest the presence of a preclinical form of the disease (Arriagada *et al.*, 1992).

Table 4.1 lists the many anatomic and pathologic features that together form the tapestry of the aging healthy brain. While most authorities regard lesions in the left column as benign and without functional consequences, the same is not true for pathologic lesions tabulated in the right column.

Anatomic 'benign' lesions

White matter granular degeneration

In virtually all persons who die after age 50 years, the white matter (WM) exhibits widespread 'granular degeneration' (**4.2**) when stained with an antibody to ubiquitin (Wang *et al.*, 2004). Nearby corpora amylacea (see below) are also ubiquinated. The granules are intimately associated with myelin bundles. The common interpretation among neuropathologists is that this is a universal accompaniment of aging in the human brain. So far, no specific pathologic or functional significance has been attached to the morphologic phenomenon.

Neuronal lipofuscin

Intracellular accumulation of this proteolipid material in secondary lysosomes is a recognized valid correlate of chronological age in both vertebrates and invertebrates (Brunk & Terman, 2002). In the former, lipofuscin pigment accumulates in myocardial cells, hepatocytes, and central neurons (**4.3**). Lipofuscin levels in the superior temporal gyrus do not differ between nondemented controls and AD patients (Mountjoy *et al.*, 2005).

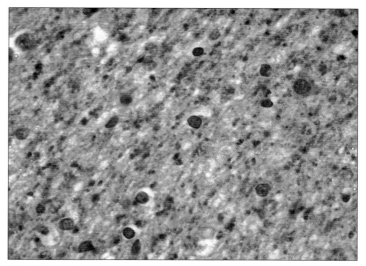

4.2 Ubiquitin antibody localizes to white matter myelin as punctate brown dots, a lesion that is referred to as 'granular degeneration of myelin'. The lesion is almost universal after 50 years of age in persons with no clinically evident neurologic dysfunction. (×40 objective.)

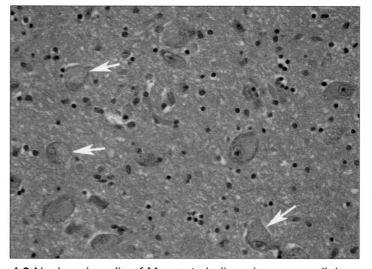

4.3 Nucleus basalis of Meynert cholinergic magnocellular neurons, similar to many others in the human brain, accumulate lipofuscin lipopigment (arrows) as a direct consequence of chronologic aging. The brown pigment represents degraded proteolipids in secondary lysosomes that cannot be entirely digested by acid hydrolases. Lipofuscin pigment appears lighter and finer in texture than neuromelanin, which has a different biochemical composition. (H&E, ×20 objective.)

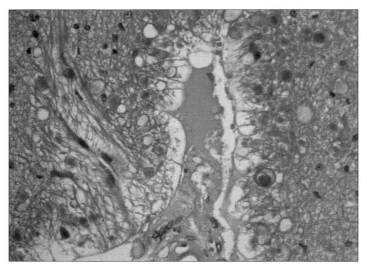

4.4. Corpora amylacea are round structures formed mostly of glucose polymers. They cluster in white matter around blood vessels, near ependymal surfaces, and at the subpial glia limitans, where formation by astrocytes can be visualized. (H&E, ×20 objective.)

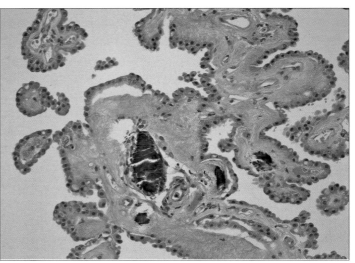

4.5 Choroid plexus blood vessels and connective tissue matrix are prone to develop dystrophic calcification as a function of aging. Such lesions are often visualized as dense areas on MRI and CT brain scans. (H&E, ×1 objective.)

Corpora amylacea (CA)

These bodies of polymerized glucose form in astrocytes and are deposited around ventricular surfaces (**4.4**) (Mrak *et al.*, 1997). CA also occur in the WM fiber tracts and in the subpial membrane. Formerly regarded as completely benign, abnormal CA build-up is now recognized to occur in certain pathologic situations including the temporal lobes of person undergoing resection for intractable temporal lobe epilepsy (Chung & Horoupian, 1996). It has been proposed that CA act as protective traps or sinks for damaged molecules since the core (~4% protein) contains a variety of partly degraded proteins (Cavanagh, 1999). Ubiquitin is a strong biomarker for CA, for example.

Calcification of the choroid plexus (CP)

CP function declines as a function of aging (Rubenstein, 1998); however, the anatomic and biochemical bases for this are not well understood. Neuroradiologists and morphologists are well aware that the CP develops progressive calcification during normal healthy aging (**4.5**). Coincident with interstitial calcification, CP arteries exhibit collagen fibrous replacement, often referred to as 'hyalinization', of their walls.

Ferruginization of cerebral arteries

Cerebral arteries in the basal ganglia, thalamus, and cerebellar WM are prone to develop mural deposits of calcium and iron with aging (**4.6**). Usually this is a focal and incidental finding of no established clinical significance. It is unclear why these particular blood vessels develop dystrophic calcification and iron deposition. Small arteries and arterioles in the end plate region of the hippocampus also occasionally become calcified in a similar fashion.

Up-regulation of the glial acid fibrillary protein (GFAP) messenger RNA and protein

A number of studies have documented that GFAP mRNA and the GFAP intermediate filament protein of astrocytes are up-regulated during normal aging in the mouse and human brain (Nichols *et al.*, 1993). The precise biochemical basis for this change is not known. It is possible that GFAP increases as part of a general 'gliosis' that accompanies multifocal neuronal loss but this theory has not yet been substantiated. Gliosis is further discussed in Chapter 5 (**5.21**; Schechter *et al.*, 1981).

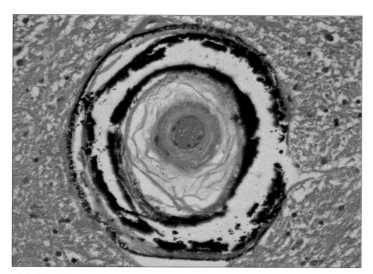

4.6 Arteries in the thalamus, cerebellum, and basal ganglia such as this one in the nucleus accumbens accumulate aging-associated dystrophic mural deposits of calcium and iron salts that may be visualized with ordinary H&E or Perl's iron stain. (×20 objective.)

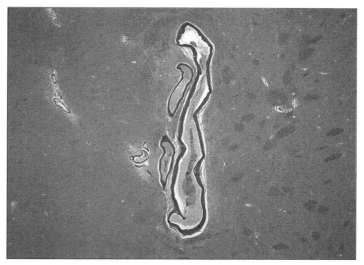

4.7 A deep white collection of blood vessel profiles is consistent with a three dimensional tortuous course, where vascular loops have been cross-sectioned several times within a 6 μm histologic section (see Nonaka *et al.*, 2003). (H&E, ×1 objective.)

Widening of Virchow–Robins perivascular spaces

Nonaka *et al.* (1993) have shown a dramatic increase in WM vascular tortuosity in the aging brain. In fact, micro-angiographic studies combined with scanning electron microscopy have shown that certain blood vessels develop twisted pretzel-like 'knots.' The consequence is a widening of the surrounding perivascular spaces to accommodate the widened vascular loops. This change can be detected in ordinary H&E sections (**4.7**).

The posterior subputamenal region brain is often the site of dramatically widened Virchow–Robins spaces seen by magnetic resonance imaging (MRI) and on gross examination. Experienced neuroradiologists recognize these lesions as a normal anatomic variant, but less experienced diagnosticians may occasionally mistake large ones for lacunar infarcts or small hemorrhagic foci.

Meningeal fibrosis

The leptomeninges at the vertex of the cerebral hemispheres develop aging-related circumscribed collagen fibrosis that conforms to the area bounded when the touching thumbs and middle fingers of both hands are placed over the vertex (**4.8**). This can be a useful 'rule of thumb' guideline since meningeal fibrosis may be mistaken at autopsy for purulent exudate indicative of an acute bacterial meningitis.

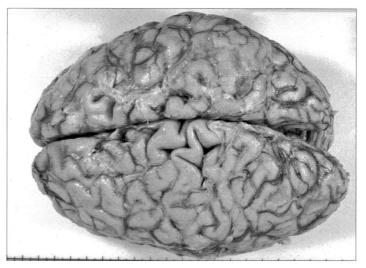

4.8 The dorsum of brains of individuals beyond age 40 years progressively develop localized fibrous opacification of the meninges over the vertex of the cerebrum as a function of aging. This normal finding should not be confused with the accumulation of yellow-green purulent material in cases of acute bacterial meningitis.

Frontal horn ventricular rounding

Experience observing more than 1,020 histologically studied brains from nondemented and demented individuals in the Alzheimer's Disease Research Center (ADRC) registry provide convincing evidence that pathologic ventricular enlargement in persons with mild AD is often labeled as 'ventricular enlargement appropriate for age' by radiologists. The intent appears to be to not unduly alarm patients but this may be misleading and unfair as evidence continues to build that medial temporal and frontal atrophy occur early in the course of AD, including the preclinical phase (Fotenos *et al.*, 2005). Good intentions do not necessarily make good science! A better approach would be to develop (or apply existing) objective criteria for scoring brain atrophy and ventricular dilatation and to apply them routinely to structural MRI scans on nondemented elderly persons. The author developed one such method with neuroradiologist Mokhtar Gado, MD (see *Box 5.3*, p. 80) (McKeel & Gado, 1994), and a parallel method was developed for antemortem MRI structural studies with cognitive neuropsychologist Randy Buckner, PhD, at Washington University (*Box 4.2*).

Periventricular myelin pallor (scan 'caps' and 'high signal areas')

Brain scans (computed tomography [CT], MRI) from elderly nondemented patients frequently reveal WM lesions (WMLs) that are both periventricular and deep. An exact histopathologic correlate of these often dramatic MRI appearances has not emerged. Periventricular 'caps' on MRI correspond to areas that by H&E screening stain and LFB-PAS myelin stain conform to WM areas of 'pallor' where myelinated fibers are spread apart, may be pale, and are frequently associated with thickened blood vessels with hyalinized acellular walls (Morris *et al.*, 1990). Inflammatory cells and macrophages are usually inconspicuous in such areas. Many investigators believe the primary lesion in such areas of pallor is focal cerebral edema. Subependymal blood vessels, for example in the caudate nucleus, undergo similar hyaline mural thickening surrounded by widened perivascular spaces (**4.9**).

Deeper mild WMLs may show edema or a lesion that Brun and Englund called 'incomplete infarction' (1986). Besides edema and pallor, WM contains some macrophages and a diminished number of oligodendrocytes, which the

---

Box 4.2 MRI brain atrophy and aging

Structural T1 weighted brain magnetic resonance image (MRI) scans provide excellent anatomic correlation during life with postmortem atrophy scores (compare with *Box 5.3*, p. 80). Gray and white matter and the cerebral ventricular system size may be assessed. Row 1 includes MRI images from a normal college-aged person. The angles of the frontal horns are razor sharp (left column), the body of the ventricle is small (middle column), and the ventricular trigone (right column) is also very small. The middle and lower rows display progressive degrees of cerebral atrophy and ventricular dilatation seen in Alzheimer patients. The number to the left is the atrophy/ventricular size score to compare with the anatomic visual standards (*Box 5.3*, p. 80). Grades 2 and 3 show progressive gyral gray matter thinning, sulcal widening, hippocampal atrophy, and white matter loss in addition to the ventricular size alterations.

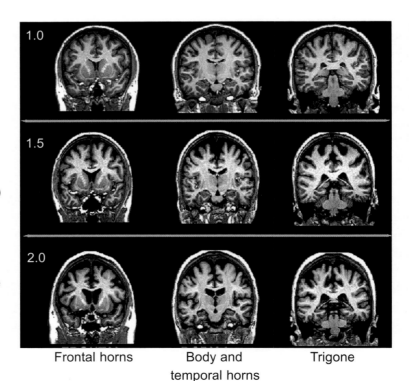

Frontal horns   Body and   Trigone
                    temporal horns

Scandinavian authors believe represent subinfarctive ischemic lesions. Acceptance of the incomplete infarction theory of deep WMLs is not universal because several careful studies in which lesion-bearing MRI regions were examined histologically have shown only edema rather than tissue ischemic necrosis (Scheltens *et al.*, 1995). In addition, clinical stroke history has been reported to correlate poorly with WMLs on MRI or CT scans.

From this pathologist's experience, the overwhelming majority of WMLs seen on MRI appear to represent WM edema primarily when the brain is viewed at autopsy. Grossly, no pathology is seen in the usual case regardless of the 'severity' (number, spatial extent) of the WMLs. The exception at the microscopic level is that periventricular blood vessels in the regions of MRI WM 'caps' have thickened, acellular, fibrotic ('hyaline change') walls (**4.10**). This vascular change is almost universal after about age 50 years. The age when this fibrohyalinosis of periventricular vasculature begins has not yet been precisely defined.

Pathologic lesions

Aging related neurofibrillary tangles (NFTs) in selected brain regions

Evidence exists that NFTs occur in certain brain regions: entorhinal cortex layer II (ERC-II) (Price *et al.*, 1991), nucleus basalis of Meynert (NBM) (Beach *et al.*, 1998), locus ceruleus (LC) (DW McKeel, Jr, unpublished data), and anterior olfactory nucleus (AON) (Price *et al.*, 1991), as a function of normal aging in the absence of Alzheimer type plaques (**4.11**). The work group that formulated the National Institute on Aging (NIA)-Reagan Institute criteria for diagnosing AD (1997) stated that even a single NFT should be regarded as pathologic. The real issue is whether or not NFTs occur as isolated lesions as an integral part of the aging process, or, are NFTs in the above regions a harbinger of AD that appears in a discordant temporal sequence before the appearance of SPs in the neocortex?

Experience at the authors' ADRC confirms that a few

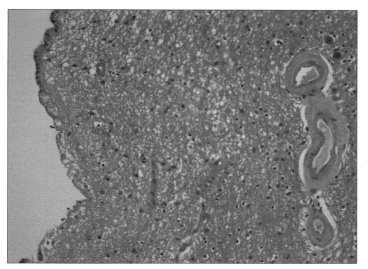

4.9 Subependymal (lumen at the left) blood vessel walls, difficult to identify as either arteries or veins, in aging brains are routinely acellular with thickened fibrous walls. (H&E, ×10 objective.)

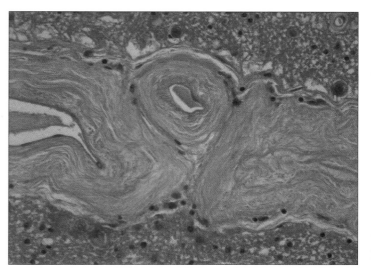

4.10 A deep centrum semiovale white matter blood vessel shows remarkable thickening and dense, nearly acellular walls that consist of collagen bundles. The process is similar to that shown in **4.9**, but is more extreme. (H&E, ×10 objective.)

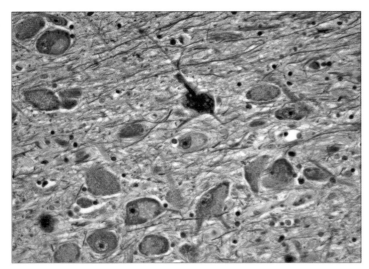

4.11 Isolated argyrophilic neurofibrillary tangles are a common autopsy finding in the nucleus basalis of Meynert after age 50 years, even in nondemented persons. The nearby neuronal population appears normal. (Modified Bielschowsky silver method, ×20 objective.)

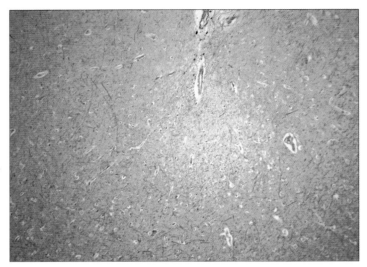

4.12 A silver stain fails to show any senile plaques or neurofibrillary tangles in the superior temporal cerebral neocortex of this 86-year-old nondemented man. (Modified Bielschowsky silver method, ×10 objective.)

tangles are often seen in ERC-II, NBM, AON, LC, and the substantia nigra (SN) of nondemented controls that are rated CDR 0 at death. Neuropil threads (NT) co-occur in small numbers with NFTs in ERC-II, LC, and SN (Braak et al., 1986).

Isolated preamyloid and diffuse senile plaques

The most controversial issue in diagnosing Alzheimer's disease using pathologic criteria is the clinical importance of non-neuritic senile plaques (NNSPs) in the brains of nondemented elderly individuals. Extensive data on nondemented elderly brains has been obtained at the authors' center (Price & Morris, 1999 [39 brains]; Morris et al., 1996 [21 brains]; Price et al., 2001 [39 brains]; DW McKeel, Jr and NS Havlioglu 'decades study' [104 institutional controls, unpublished data]) and in collaboration with six other ADRCs (Morris et al., 2004). These studies collectively indicate there are three basic classes of AD type neuropathology that characterize nondemented aging as described below.

About 60% of brains from persons who are 70 years or more at death have no demonstrable argyrophilic (silver positive) or a-beta immunoreactive (Aβ-IR) plaque-like deposits in either the neocortex (**4.12**) or hippocampus. The

stellate neurons that comprise the ERC-II and the most medial segment of hippocampal CA1 (the 'initial segment') almost always contain a few neurofibrillary pretangles and intraneuronal tangles that are staged as Braak I–II (Braak and Braak, 1991). In the authors' experience NFTs in ERC-II and CA1 are first seen during the sixth decade (50–60 years) (NS Havlioglu and DW McKeel, Jr, unpublished data). Persons dying at younger ages may have no demonstrable NFTs in the same brain regions (Braak stage 0).

A few SPs may be detected using a-beta antibodies and the Hedreen–Bielschowsky silver method in many brains with zero or only a few isolated NFTs (**4.13**). These are the authors' ADRC's most sensitive lesion detection methods. Thus, NFTs rarely occur in total isolation in the vulnerable regions discussed in this chapter. SP burden, however, may be very low and individual SPs or small SP clusters may be spread far apart in the voluminous, highly folded cerebral cortex. Preamyloid SPs (Tagliavini et al., 1988) by definition are labeled with a-beta antibodies but fail to stain with silver, thioflavine S, or Congo red. As a result, unless a-beta immunohistochemistry is used, preamyloid plaques that precede, or coincide with, formation of both diffuse and neuritic SPs will fail to be detected.

A minority (25–40%, Morris et al., 2004) of brains from

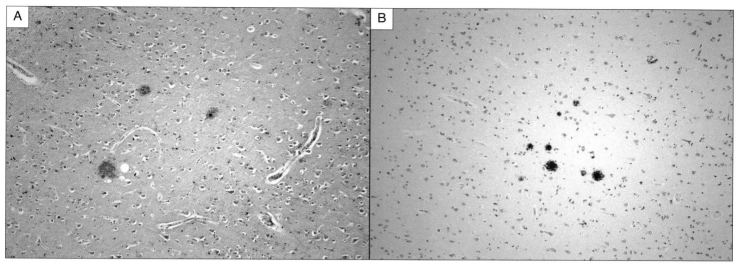

4.13 The superior temporal cortex of a 87-year-old nondemented man displays patchy diffuse senile plaques (SP) in both modified Bielschowsky silver (**A**) and amyloid beta (a-beta) immunohistochemical stains (brown peroxidase substrate) (**B**). In contrast to diffuse SP, preamyloid plaques, had they been present, would stain only with a-beta antibody but not with silver methods. (×10 objective for both panels.)

nondemented elderly persons 70–100+ years of age at death have both SPs and NFTs in the distribution pattern that characterizes brains from very mildly cognitively impaired (i.e. CDR 0.5) AD patients and persons with mild cognitive impairment (MCI) in the memory domain (**4.14**) (Petersen, 2004). The authors regard these people as having preclinical AD since 70% will progress to mild (CDR 1) AD within 2 years (Goldman *et al.*, 2001). The detailed presentation of preclinical pathologic AD is contained in Chapter 5 on the neuropathology of clinically overt AD.

One may wonder why it appears so difficult for pathologists to agree on a universal definition of AD in all its stages. Pathologists commonly examine one histologic section with a dimension of approximately 0.8 inches × 0.8 inches × 6 μm thick for each cerebral lobe. One to four such sections thus routinely constitutes the 'neocortical' sample. Accordingly, small numbers of cortical plaques or isolated tangles (or any other dispersed lesion) could be easily missed using such a sampling scheme. It is therefore the authors' opinion that 'isolated' tangles and sparse SP may constitute the earliest demonstrable lesion profile of the earliest anatomic expression of AD. A high density unbiased sampling study would be necessary to determine more definitively whether SPs or NFTs appear first.

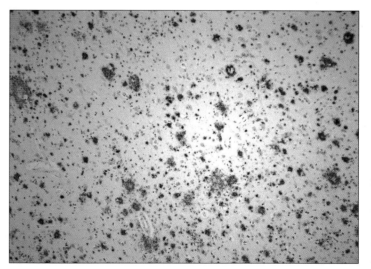

4.14 Prefrontal cortex of an 82-year-old very mildly demented (CDR 0.5) woman contains widespread dense beta-amyloid deposits but only rare neurofibrillary tau-positive tangles or tau-positive neuropil threads. (Dual immunohistochemistry with antibodies to beta amyloid [red substrate] and hyperphosphorylated tau [blue-black substrate], ×10 objective.)

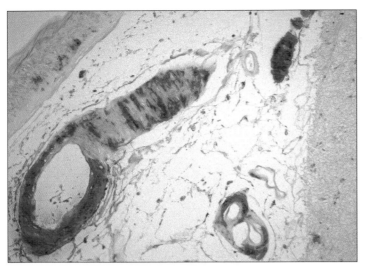

4.15 Leptomeningeal large and smaller arteries of this 90-year-old woman stain intensely with beta-amyloid antibody and a red substrate. (Dual immuno-histochemistry with antibodies to beta amyloid [red substrate] and hyperphosphorylated tau [blue-black substrate], ×10 objective.)

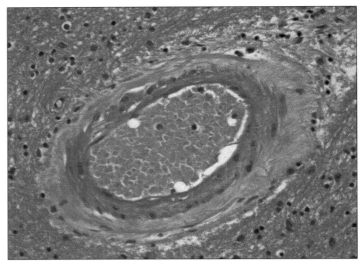

4.16 A deep white matter artery shows mural thickening with prominent outer medial and adventitial fibrosis, the so-called lipohyaline change. Such vessels often display perivascular hemosiderin macrophages, indicating bleeding has occurred. A few chronic inflammatory cells are also commonly present around such arteries. (H&E, ×20 objective.)

Isolated cerebral amyloid angiopathy (CAA)

Focal deposits of a-beta peptide in leptomeningeal arteries are relatively common in brains of nondemented elderly persons (**4.15**). The occurrence rate is 10–30% in various reported series (Revesz et al., 2003). The reported prevalence of CAA is partly influenced by the method used to detect vascular amyloid. Precise comparative performance data of Congo red, thioflavine S, Gallyas silver, and a-beta immunohistochemistry to detect CAA are not available. In the authors' experience, Congo red is least sensitive, while the other three methods have roughly comparable sensitivity to detect cerebral beta amyloid deposits. The fact that elderly persons with isolated CAA developed lobar cerebral hemorrhages (Izumihara et al., 2005) is evidence that CAA, in the absence of AD, is a potentially serious condition rather than being a benign lesion. CAA should also be regarded as aging-associated rather than being a direct effect of aging. This interpretation is supported by the fact that a large majority of elderly persons do not have demonstrable CAA in routine autopsy brain sections.

Arterial lipohyalinosis

Cerebral arteries undergo a series of histopathologic changes as part of normal aging. These changes must be distinguished from the effects of vascular risk factors, most importantly hypertension and diabetes mellitus. The vascular wall of certain blood vessels may lose smooth muscle cells and undergo replacement fibrosis (**4.16**) (Thal et al., 2003). Arterial lipohyalinosis is a more specific vascular lesion that is exacerbated by hypertension and aging. Affected arteries develop foamy macrophages as well as fibrosis.

Lacunar infarction

No one doubts that small lacunar infarcts (<1.5 cm as originally described by CM Fisher [1965]) are pathologic lesions. However, they are so common in certain regions such as the thalamus, caudate, and putamen that some regard them as 'aging'-related lesions.

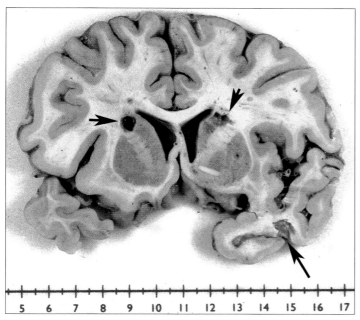

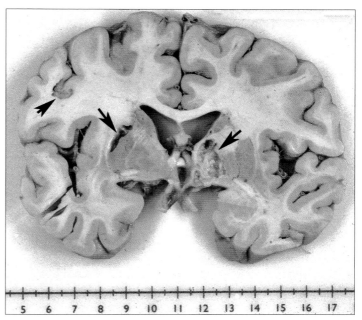

4.17 A coronal section through the brain of a 90-year-old female (CDR 0.5 at death, apolipoprotein E genotype ε24) had 19 macroscopically identifiable infarcts throughout her cerebrum. The arrows point to small infarcts in both caudate nuclei and a part of the inferior temporal cortex. (Formalin fixed autopsy specimen.)

4.18 A coronal slide 1 cm behind **4.17** reveals large infarcts that destroyed the right hypothalamus. The opposite putamen has a large slit-like infarct. The cortex also has a small infarct (arrows). (Formalin fixed autopsy specimen.)

A case example illustrates why interpretation of small vascular lesions in the aging brain is so difficult. A 90-year-old woman had very mild CDR 0.5 dementia during life but had 19 discrete infarcts in her brain at autopsy (**4.17**). Her apolipoprotien E (apoE) genotype was 24. Sparse neocortical diffuse SPs were detected (see **4.13**). One such lesion destroyed the hypothalamus and one mammillary body (**4.18**), and probably contributed to her death. Microscopic examination revealed both focal subacute lesions with gitter macrophages and perilesional reactive astrocytosis (**4.19**), together with small remote cavitary lesions.

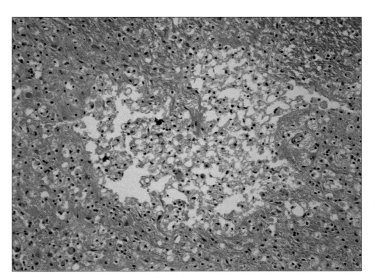

4.19 A small, sharply defined white matter subacute infarct is characterized by tissue destruction with loss of both myelin and axons. The demarcating cavity is filled with foamy macrophages ('gitter' cells). Had this lesion progressed, a cavitary 'lacune' would have ensued. (H&E, ×10 objective.)

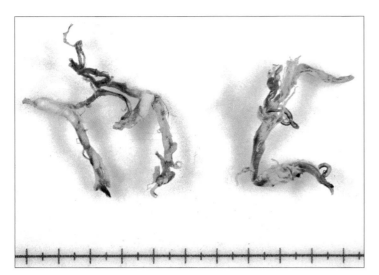

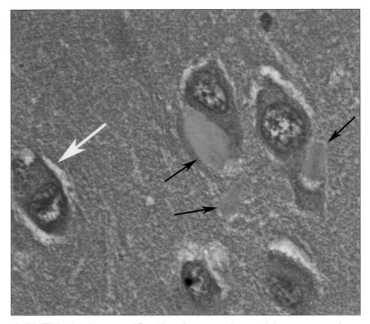

4.20 The arterial circle of Willis has been dissected away from the base of the brain at autopsy. The anterior circulation is at left and the posterior vertebrobasilar circulation is at right. Note the preferential involvement of anterior arteries by yellow nonoccluding atherosclerotic plaques. The autopsy specimen is from the same patient's brain portrayed in **4.18** and **4.19**.

4.21 This high magnification image shows hippocampal CA1 neurons with two distinct age-associated lesions. Granulovacuolar degeneration (yellow arrow) presents as cytoplasmic clear zones containing a denser granule. Such regions of the cell sequester tubulin and caspase-3 as well as other cytoskeletal elements (autophagocytosis). The three black arrows point to individual Hirano bodies, actin paracrystalline lattices that form within, and are enveloped by, neuronal plasma membranes. Both lesions increase in number and spatial distribution in Alzheimer's disease compared to normal aging (see Woodard, 1962; Fisher, 1965; Selznick *et al.*, 1999). (H&E, x40 objective.)

Atherosclerosis of the arterial circle of Willis

Atherosclerosis is a pathologic aging-associated process whereby foamy lipid-rich macrophages and smooth muscle cells build up in the walls of large cerebral arteries. The arterial circle of Willis at the base of the brain and its arterial tributaries develop segmental, regional, and diffuse disease (**4.20**). Such atherosclerotic plaques, when the lumen is compromised greater than about 75%, may lead to occlusive reductions of blood flow (see **4.1**). The result is either transient infarction with minimal or no lasting clinical sequelae (transient ischemic attacks, TIAs), or completed ischemic infarcts (strokes) with permanent destruction of brain tissue.

Hippocampal CA1 granulovacuolar degeneration (GVD)

Pyramidal neuronal cells of the hippocampal CA1 field develop a cytoplasmic lesion termed GVD that consists of a clear vacuole, in the center of which is a dense granule (**4.21**). The dense granules are labeled with antibodies to tubulin, tau, and activated caspase-3 (Selznick *et al.*, 1999). Two studies (Woodard, 1962; Tomlinson and Kitchener, 1972) have shown that up to 9% of CA1 neurons may be affected in nondemented individuals. In contrast, they as well as Ball (1978) have shown that GVD prevalences higher than 9% are strongly correlated with NFTs and related AD pathologic lesions.

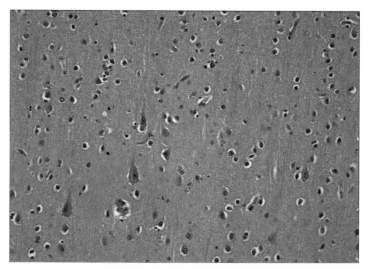

4.22 Superior temporal neocortex from a 91-year-old apolipoprotein E ε33 genotype woman shows nearly normal appearing neuronal and glial histology, even though she was moderately demented at the time of death. (H&E, ×10 objective.)

Cortical atrophy

Dekaban showed in 1978, based on autopsy brain weights of over 2,400 men and 2,300 women, that the human brains loses mass at the rate of about 0.2% per decade beginning at age 50–55 years. Modern MRI volumetric studies have confirmed that cortical gray matter loss occurs at about this same rate in nondemented persons as a function of age. Atrophy rates that are higher may herald the presence of incipient dementia (Fotenos *et al.*, 2005), as discussed further in Chapter 5 on the neuropathology of preclinical and overt AD.

Ventricular enlargement

Data from Kaye's group (Mueller *et al.*, 1998) and from the authors' center indicate that cognitively defined persons who are CDR 0 have near normal sized cerebral ventricular systems through their 90s. Coronal sections reveal slight rounding of the frontal horn lateral angles, mild enlargement of the temporal horns with slight hippocampal atrophy, and near normal sized ventricular bodies and trigonal areas. Such brains are represented in row 1 of *Box 4.2*. When greater degrees of sulcal widening and ventricular enlargement are encountered as shown in rows 2 and 3 of *Box 4.2*, an incipient or established dementing disorder should be suspected as the underlying cause.

Selective neuronal loss

Studies by Brody (1955) and others indicated that perhaps 50% of cortical neurons were lost as part of normal brain aging. Beginning in the 1970s with quantitative image analysis studies and continuing with the application of unbiased stereologic quantification of human neuronal populations, it has become clear that age-associated neuronal loss in the human brain is highly selective and certainly is of lesser overall magnitude than the Brody studies had indicated (**4.22**). For example, quantitative morphometric analysis indicates that LC pigmented noradrenergic neurons are lost during aging (Lohr & Jeste, 1988), whereas superior temporal sulcus (Gómez-Isla *et al.*, 1997) and ERC-II (Gómez-Isla *et al.*, 1996) and hippocampal CA1 neurons are well maintained in cognitively intact persons up to their 90s (Price *et al.*, 2001).

As will be seen in the following chapter on AD, the borderline between normal healthy brain aging and early AD dementing disease is still being defined clinically, psychometrically, by neuroimaging modalities, and by neuropathology. This challenging task is hindered by a lack of precise criteria for diagnosing the earliest manifestations of AD.

References

Arriagada PV, Marzloff K, Hyman BT (1992). Distribution of Alzheimer-type pathologic changes in nondemented elderly individuals matches the pattern in Alzheimer's disease. *Neurology* **42**:1681–1688.

Ball MJ (1978). Topographic distribution of neurofibrillary tangles and granulovacuolar degeneration in hippocampal cortex of aging and demented patients. A quantitative study. *Acta Neuropathol* **42**:73–80.

Beach TG, Sue LI, Scott S, et al. (1998). Neurofibrillary tangles are constant in aging human nucleus basalis. *Alzheimer's Rep.* **6**:375–380.

Braak H, Braak E (1991). The neuropathologic stageing of Alzheimer-related changes. *Acta Neuropathol.* (Berlin) **82**:239–259.

Braak H, Braak E, Grundke-Iqbal I, et al. (1986). Occurrence of neuropil threads in the senile human brain and in Alzheimer's disease: a third location of paired helical filaments outside of neurofibrillary tangles and neuritic plaques. *Neurosci. Lett.* **65**:351–355.

Brody H (1955). Organization of the cerebral cortex. III. A study of aging in the human cerebral cortex. *J. Comp. Neurol.* **102**:511–516.

Brun A, Englund E (1986). A white matter disorder in dementia of the Alzheimer type: a pathoanatomical study. *Ann. Neurol.* **19**:253–262.

Brunk UT, Terman A (2002). Lipofuscin: mechanisms of age-related accumulation and influence on cell function. (Review) (75 refs). *Free Radical Biology & Medicine* **33**:611–619.

Cavanagh JB (1999). Corpora amylacea and the family of polyglucosan diseases. (Review) (235 refs). *Brain Res. Rev.* **29**:265–295.

Chung MH. Horoupian DS (1996). Corpora amylacea: a marker for mesial temporal sclerosis. *J. Neuropathol. Exp. Neurol.* **55**:403–408.

Dekaban AS (1978). Changes in brain weights during the span of human life: relation of brain weights to body heights and body weights. *Ann. Neurol.* **4**:345–356.

Fisher CM (1965). Lacune: small deep cerebral infarcts. *Neurology* **15**:774–784.

Fotenos AF, Snyder AZ, Girton LE, et al. (2005). Normative estimates of cross-sectional and longitudinal brain volume decline in aging and AD. *Neurology* **64**:1032–1039.

Franks LM (1954). Latent carcinoma of the prostate. *J. Pathol. Bacteriol.* **68**:603–616.

Goldman WP, Storandt M, Miller JP, et al. (2001). Mild cognitive impairment represents early-stage Alzheimer's disease. *Arch. Neurol.* **58**:397–405.

Gómez-Isla T, Hollister R, West H, et al. (1997). Neuronal loss correlates with but exceeds neurofibrillary tangles in Alzheimer's disease. *Ann. Neurol.* **41**:17–24.

Gómez-Isla T, Price JL, McKeel DW Jr, et al. (1996). Profound loss of layer II entorhinal cortex neurons in very mild Alzheimer's disease. *J. Neurosci.* **16**:4491–4500.

Izumihara A, Suzuki M, Ishihara T (2005). Recurrence and extension of lobar hemorrhage related to cerebral amyloid angiopathy: multivariate analysis of clinical risk factors. *Surg. Neurol.* **64**:160–164.

Lohr JB, Jeste DV (1988). Locus ceruleus morphometry in aging and schizophrenia. (Review) (48 refs). *Acta Psych. Scand.* **77**:689–697.

McKeel DW Jr, Gado M (1994). A visual standards based system for scoring Alzheimer and aging-related human brain atrophy at autopsy (abstr. P34-11). *Brain Pathol.* **4**:544.

Morris JC, Gado M, Torack RM, et al. (1990). Binswanger's disease or artifact: a clinical, neuroimaging, and pathological study of periventricular white matter changes in Alzheimer's disease. *Adv. Neurol.* **51**:47–52.

Morris JC, Hurst E, McKeel DW Jr, et al. (2000). Healthy brain aging in nonagenarians and centenarians. *World Congress of Neurology* July.

Morris JC, McKeel DW Jr, Buckles VD, et al. (2004). Neuropathological markers of preclinical Alzheimer's disease in nondemented aging. *J. Neurosci. Abstr.* **902**:16; online (URL: http://sfn.scholarone.com/itin2004/index.html).

Morris JC, Storandt M, McKeel DW Jr, et al. (1996). Cerebral amyloid deposition and diffuse plaques in 'normal' aging: evidence for presymptomatic and very mild Alzheimer's disease. *Neurology* **46**:707–719.

Mountjoy CQ, Dowson JH, Harrington C, et al. (2005). Characteristics of neuronal lipofuscin in the superior temporal gyrus in Alzheimer's disease do not differ from nondiseased controls: a comparison with disease-related changes in the superior frontal gyrus. *Acta Neuropathol.* **109**:490–496.

Mrak RE, Griffin ST, Graham DI 91997). Aging-associated changes in human brain. (Review) (60 refs). *J. Neuropathol. Exp. Neurol.* **56**:1269–1275.

Mueller EA, Moore MM, Kerr DC, *et al.* (1998). Brain volume preserved in healthy elderly through the eleventh decade. *Neurology* **51**:1555–1562.

NIA-Reagan Institute Working Group on Diagnostic Criteria for Neuropathological Assessment of Alzheimer's disease (1997). Working Group consensus recommendations for the postmortem diagnosis of Alzheimer's disease. *Neurobiol. Aging* **18**(Suppl 4):S1–S2.

Nichols NR, Day JR, Laping NJ, *et al.* (1993). GFAP mRNA increases with age in rat and human brain. *Neurobiol Aging* **14**:421–429.

Nonaka H, Akima M, Hatori T, *et al.* (2003). The microvasculature of the cerebral white matter: arteries of the subcortical white matter. *J. Neuropathol. Exp. Neurol.* **62**:154–161.

Petersen RC (2004). Mild cognitive impairment as a diagnostic entity. (Review) (50 refs). *J. Int. Med.* **256**:183–194.

Price JL, Davis PB, Morris JC, *et al.* (1991). The distribution of tangles, plaques and related immunohistochemical markers in healthy aging and Alzheimer's disease. *Neurobiol. Aging* **12**:295–312.

Price JL, Ko AI, Wade MJ, *et al.* (2001). Neuron number in entorhinal cortex and CA1 in preclinical Alzheimer's disease. *Arch. Neurol.* **58**:1395–1402.

Price JL, Morris JC (1999). Tangles and plaques in nondemented aging and 'preclinical' Alzheimer's disease. *Ann. Neurol.* **51**:47–52.

Revesz T, Ghiso J, Lashley T, *et al.* (2003). Cerebral amyloid angiopathies: a pathologic, biochemical, and genetic view. (Review) (80 refs). *J. Neuropathol. Exp. Neurol.* **62**:885–898.

Roher AE, Esh C, Rahman A, *et al.* (2005). Atherosclerosis of cerebral arteries in Alzheimer disease. *Stroke* **35**(Suppl 1):2623–2627.

Rubenstein E (1998). Relationship of senescence of cerebrospinal fluid circulatory system to dementias of the aged. (Review) (32 refs). *Lancet* **351**:283–285.

Scheltens P, Barkhof F, Leys D, *et al.* (1995). Histopathologic correlates of white matter changes on MRI in Alzheimer's disease and normal aging. *Neurology* **45**:883–888.

Selznick LA, Holtzman DM, Han BH, *et al.* (1999). *In situ* immunodetection of neuronal caspase-3 activation in Alzheimer disease. *J. Neuropathol. Exp. Neurol.* **58**:1020–1026.

Tagliavini F, Giaccone G, Frangione B, *et al.* (1988). Preamyloid deposits in the cerebral cortex of patients with Alzheimer's disease and nondemented individuals. *Neurosci. Lett.* **93**:191–196.

Thal DR, Ghebremedhin E, Orantes M, *et al.* (2003). Vascular pathology in Alzheimer disease: correlation of cerebral amyloid angiopathy and arteriosclerosis/lipo-hyalinosis with cognitive decline. *J. Neuropathol. Exp. Neurol.* **62**:1287–1301.

Tomlinson BE, Kitchener D (1972). Granulovacuolar degeneration of hippocampal pyramidal cells. *J. Pathol.* **106**:165–185.

Wang DS, Bennett DA, Mufson EJ, *et al.* (2004). Contribution of changes in ubiquitin and myelin basic protein to age-related cognitive decline. *Neurosci. Res.* **48**:93–100.

Woodard JS (1962). Clinicopathologic significance of granulovacuolar degeneration in Alzheimer's disease. *J. Neuropathol. Exp. Neurol.* **21**:85–91.

Chapter 5

Neuropathology of preclinical and clinical Alzheimer's disease

Introduction

Alzheimer's disease (AD) represents a tremendous public health burden as it accounts for 50–70% of cases of dementia and is by far the most common form of dementia. 20 million individuals worldwide are afflicted with AD, 4 million in the US. Incident cases of AD are expected to nearly triple in the US over the next 50 years (Hebert *et al.*, 2001). As the prevalence of AD doubles every 5 years after the age of 65 years, reaching nearly 50% in those aged over 85 years (Ebly *et al.*, 1994), the significance of AD worldwide will only increase as life expectancy improves and the population ages.

Clinical features

Table 5.1 presents the common symptoms of early AD. Short-term memory impairment is the hallmark of early AD. Common early manifestations of memory decline include forgetfulness of recent conversations, repetition of questions, and missing appointments. Early memory impairment is often accompanied by executive dysfunction leading to problems in planning and organizing. These cognitive deficits are responsible for progressive impairment in activities of daily living such as driving, shopping, managing finances, and cooking. With disease progression, impairment in other cognitive domains such as language,

Table 5.1 Common symptoms of early Alzheimer's disease

Memory loss
- Forgetful of pertinent details of recent events
- Repeating questions
- Misplacement of items

Executive dysfunction
- Difficulties managing checkbook/household finances
- Decline in cooking skills
- Decline in home repair/maintenance skills
- Trouble operating household appliances (microwave, TV remote control, telephone)

Daily activities
- Impaired performance in hobbies (playing cards, reading)
- Difficulty driving (getting lost, indecisiveness, minor or major accidents)
- Shopping (frequent trips for forgotten items, doubling up on items)

visuospatial function, calculations, and praxis becomes apparent. AD results in progressive disability, dependency, and eventually death. The mean survival after AD symptom onset is 10.3 years but may range from 2 to more than 20 years (Mendez & Cummings, 2003).

Clinical diagnostic criteria

While confirmation of the diagnosis of AD rests on neuropathologic observations after death, increasing knowledge about the clinical and behavioral symptoms of AD have improved the ability to identify AD with high accuracy (90% or higher in autopsy confirmed series from dementia research centers) (Berg et al., 1998). The diagnosis of AD has been standardized with criteria developed by the Work Group of the National Institute of Neurologic and Communicative Disorders and Stroke and the Alzheimer's Disease and Related Disorders Association (NINCDS-ADRDA).

The NINCDS-ADRDA criteria (McKhann et al., 1984) established three levels of confidence for the diagnosis of AD: probable, possible, and definite (*Table 5.2*). Definite AD can only be diagnosed by autopsy. Probable AD is diagnosed 'if there is a typical insidious onset of dementia with progression and if there are no other systemic or brain diseases that could account for the progressive memory and other cognitive deficits'. Possible AD is diagnosed when there are variations in the presentation or course of dementia, such as early or disproportionate language disturbance, or when another potentially dementing disorder (e.g. stroke) is present but is not believed to be responsible for dementia. The development of standard clinical criteria has led to rapid advances in the clinicopathologic study of AD and the implementation of multi-center clinical trials.

Table 5.2 NINCDS–ADRDA criteria for Alzheimer's disease (AD)

Probable AD
- Measurable deficits in two or more areas of cognition
- No disturbance in consciousness
- Progressive worsening
- Onset between 40 and 90 years
- Absence of systemic disease or other brain disease that could account for the deficits
- Diagnostic support:
  - Progressive deterioration
  - Impaired ADLs
  - Family history of similar disorder
  - Normal LP/EEG
  - Atrophy on CT
- Other consistent clinical features include plateaus in the course of progression, associated symptoms of depression, insomnia, incontinence, delusions, illusions, sexual disorders, seizures (in advanced disease), neurologic abnormalities such as increased tone, myoclonus, gait disorders

- Features making diagnosis unlikely include sudden onset, focal neurologic signs, seizures or gait disturbance early in the course

Possible AD
- Dementia syndrome with variations in onset, course, or presentation or the presence of other problems or disorders that may produce dementia but are not considered the cause of dementia

Definite AD
- Clinical criteria met
- Histopathologic evidence present at autopsy

ADL: activities of daily living; CT: computed tomography; EEG: electroencephalogram; LP: lumbar puncture.

(McKhann et al., 1984)

Evaluation of suspected AD

The evaluation of dementia consists of a combination of five components: history taking, physical examination, psychometric testing, neuroimaging, and laboratory testing.

History

The key information needed to diagnose dementia and create a differential diagnosis comes primarily from the clinical information. Clinically diagnosing AD rests on determining whether cognitive decline is present to such a degree as to interfere with function in usual activities. Observations from an attentive family member, relative, or friend describing cognitive changes interfering even mildly with the patient's usual function are essential in making a confident diagnosis.

Physical examination

In mild and even moderate AD, focal neurologic abnormalities are infrequent. The neurologic exam is performed primarily to evaluate for the presence of any signs suggestive of another dementing illness such as focal upper motor neuron signs, extrapyramidal signs, and prominent aphasia and apraxia (*Table 5.3*). Focal neurologic deficits may indicate the presence of significant vascular disease, which commonly coexists with AD, and may play a role in the symptomatic expression of AD (Snowdon *et al.*, 1997). The presence of increased tone and a Parkinsonian gait early in the course may indicate dementia with Lewy bodies or Parkinson's dementia. Extrapyramidal signs are common in advanced AD but are generally not prominent early in the course. Prominent unilateral extrapyramidal signs may indicate corticobasal degeneration. Prominent myoclonus may indicate Creutzfeldt–Jakob disease, especially if accompanying a rapidly progressive dementing illness, although myoclonus can also be encountered in AD.

Psychometric testing

Mental status tests should be used primarily to confirm the presence of cognitive deficits and not as a method of diagnosis. Mental status tests cannot, certainly at the initial evaluation, indicate whether the individual has declined from previous levels of cognitive abilities nor determine the presence of impairment sufficient to interfere with accustomed activities. Testing is useful in demonstrating a pattern of deficits consistent with an AD pattern (primary deficits in memory and executive function) and to monitor dementia progression over time through serial testing. Over-reliance on cognitive test performance in addition to failure to incorporate an informant's observations about an individual's cognitive function in relation to past abilities results in the under-recognition of mild AD.

Neuroimaging

Structural neuroimaging is recommended in the form of either magnetic resonance imaging (MRI) or noncontrast computed tomography (CT). The basis of this recommendation is evidence that up to 5% of patients with dementia have a clinically significant structural lesion that would not have been predicted based on the history or examination (Chui & Zhang, 1997). These potential lesions include brain neoplasms, subdural hematomas, or normal pressure hydrocephalus. However, fully reversible dementia due to unsuspected causes is rare.

A number of techniques are being explored in an attempt to identify inclusionary neuroimaging findings to support the diagnosis of AD. A major thrust has been in identifying neuroanatomic changes, such as atrophy, that may predict cognitive decline related to AD. The molecular imaging of amyloid deposits has promise as a potential biomarker for AD, and possibly may allow the identification of individuals who are still in the presymptomatic stages of the illness (*Box 5.1*, overleaf).

Table 5.3 Features suggestive of other dementing illness

Parkinsonism: dementia with Lewy bodies, corticobasal degeneration

Language:
- Naming impairment: progressive nonfluent aphasia
- Comprehension impairment: semantic dementia

Apraxia: corticobasal degeneration

Myoclonus: prion disease (Creutzfeldt–Jakob disease)

Box 5.1 Imaging amyloid

The molecular imaging of amyloid deposits has promise as a potential biomarker for AD and possibly may allow the identification of individuals who are still in the presymptomatic stages of the illness (Mintun *et al.*, 2006). Radioligands have been developed that cross the blood–brain barrier and bind specifically to amyloid aggregates in sufficient amounts to be imaged by PET (Revesz *et al.*, 2003; Attems & Jellinger, 2004). These images demonstrate increased uptake of the radioligand as evident by increased signal detected using PET imaging (yellow and red signal) in an individual with AD (**A**) compared to an individual without cognitive decline (**B**). (Adapted from Mintun *et al.*, 2006).

In a proof of concept PET study, a benzothiole amyloid agent, also known as Pittsburgh compound-B (PIB), resulted in significantly higher standardized uptake values in 16 AD patients compared to 6 elderly control subjects in regions known to have extensive amyloid deposition (Izumihara *et al.*, 2005). Preferential retention of PIB in frontal and temporoparietal cortex discriminated between most mild AD individuals and control subjects. These initial results suggest that PET imaging with amyloid tracer may offer the ability to quantitate cerebral amyloid in living humans.

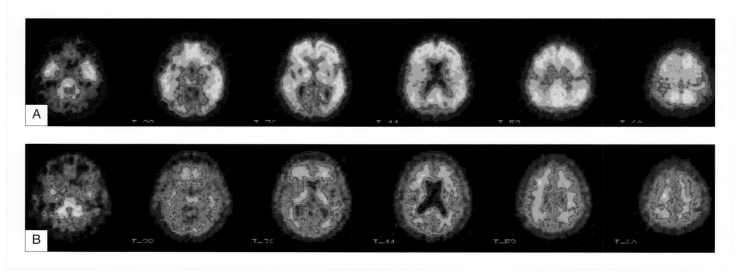

Laboratory testing

Vitamin B_{12} deficiency and hypothyroidism are common co-morbidities in patients with suspected dementia, and screening for these treatable disorders is recommended (Knopman *et al.*, 2001). A few reports have attributed dementia to B_{12} deficiency and hypothyroidism (Clarfield, 1988). In most individuals, treatment of these disorders is unlikely to completely reverse cognitive deficits and cognitive improvement in demented patients with B_{12} and thyroid replacement are equivocal (Knopman *et al.*, 2001). Nevertheless, the high frequency of these co-morbidities and the potential for amelioration of cognitive symptoms necessitates screening (*Table 5.4*). Routine screening for syphilis is no longer recommended, a change from the 1994 practice parameter (AAN, 1994) unless syphilis risk factors or evidence of infection exists.

Table 5.4 Basic laboratory assessment for cognitive impairment

Neuroimaging
- CT
- MRI

Laboratory
- Thyroid
- Vitamin B_{12}
- Syphilis (only if clinically indicated)

Pathology of normal brain aging

This topic is covered in considerably more detail in Chapter 4. A brief discussion is presented here as a prelude to discussing the neuropathology of preclinical and overt AD that follows.

A large majority of brains from nondemented persons who show no cognitive impairment at or near the time of death show minimum AD pathology regardless of the age of death. Neocortex sections reveal no, single, or small clusters of isolated a-beta deposits (**5.1**) that are often silver- and thioflavine S-negative or weakly positive. Cerebral amyloid (a-beta) angiopathy (CAA) may or may not be detected. The hippocampal medial CA1 field and entorhinal cortex layer II stellate cells (ERC-II) may show sparse to moderate neurofibrillary tangles (NFTs) that are mostly intraneuronal. Neuropil threads (NT) are often confined to ERC-II and to transitional allocortex along the descending limb of the collateral sulcus (**5.2**). Braak neurofibrillary staging (Braak & Braak, 1991) (*Box 5.2*, overleaf) is commonly in the stage I–III range. Senile plaques (SP) may be entirely absent from the subcortical regions, basal ganglia, thalamus, brainstem, and cerebellum. Sparse (one or two per section) tangles are often seen in the nucleus basalis of Meynert (NBM), substantia nigra, locus ceruleus, and the dorsal raphe (serotoninergic) nucleus of elderly nondemented (CDR 0) controls (DW McKeel, Jr, personal observation, unpublished) (**5.3**).

5.1 Scattered minute and complex 'satellite' a-beta diffuse plaques with absent neuropil threads or neurofibrillary tangles is the typical histopathologic profile in neocortex sections from autopsied nondemented (CDR 0) persons. (Dual a-beta [red] and PHFtau [black] immunohistochemistry, ×10 objective.)

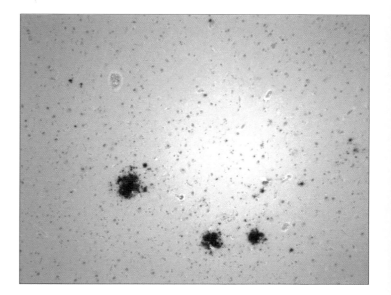

5.2 Cortex of patients with advanced (CDR 3) Alzheimer's disease harbors frequent neuritic senile plaques, neuropil threads, and neurofibrillary tangles. This pattern conforms to Braak stage V/VI (Braak & Braak, 1991). (Dual a-beta [red] and PHFtau [black] immunohistochemistry, ×20 objective.)

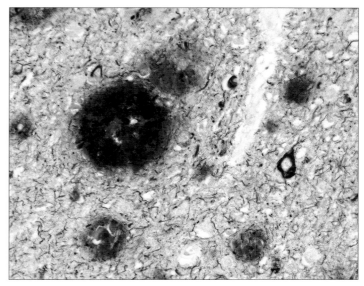

Box 5.2 Gallyas silver staging of neurofibrillary pathology in Alzheimer's disease

The system described by the Braaks (Braak & Braak, 1991) for staging neurofibrillary pathologic lesions in the Alzheimer brain is widely used worldwide. Lesions assessed in medial temporal lobe and occipital neocortex include neurofibrillary tangles, neuropil threads, and neuritic senile plaques. A score is assigned by inspection of silver or tau immunostains on brain tissue sections. Various adaptations of the original methodology have been proposed to increase the practicality of the original method. The method has wide applicability in aging and both pure and mixed forms of AD.

Stage I: Entorhinal cortex neurofibrillary tangles plus neuropil threads

Stage II: Entorhinal cortex (A35) plus hippocampal CA1 neurofibrillary tangles plus neuropil threads

Stage III: A36 lateral to collateral sulcus

Stage IV: Temporal lobe and base of brain

Stage V: Lateral and inferior lateral surface

Stage VI: Entire (holo) cortical neurofibrillary tangles plus neuropil threads

Staging on medial, temporal, and occipital sections

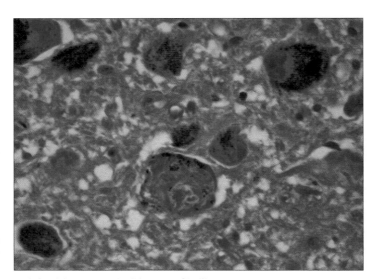

5.3 Incidental globoid neurofibrillary tangles commonly occur in small numbers in locus ceruleus (this image), dorsal raphe nucleus, and nucleus basalis of Meynert in elderly nondemented persons who exhibit no other features of Alzheimer's disease. The brown material is neuromelanin pigment. (H&E, ×40 objective.)

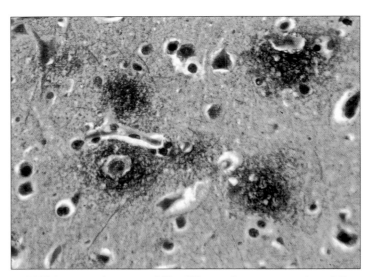

5.4 Widespread argyrophilic diffuse plaques populated the cerebrum (cortex, subcortex, cerebellum, and brainstem) of this 24-year-old nondemented (CDR 0) woman with Down's trisomy 21 syndrome. Microscopic neurofibrillary pathology was entirely absent. (Hedreen-Bielschowsky silver method, ×40 objective.)

Pathology of preclinical AD

During the past 15 years, research in a number of laboratories has indicated that the typical course of AD described above is preceded by a preclinical phase in 20–40% of nondemented individuals (Morris *et al.*, 2004). Insights into this phase of AD include those from carriers of the apolipoprotein E (apoE) epsilon 4 (ε4) allele (Arai *et al.*, 1999), from persons carrying a known mutation in amyloid precursor protein (APP), presenilin 1 (PS1) or presenilin 2 (PS2) genes that cause familial AD (FAD), and from Down's syndrome (DS) patients who carry triple copies of chromosome 21, the source of the APP gene. In DS (trisomy 21), brains from persons who die in their teens and twenties show accumulation of neocortical diffuse SP (5.4) in the absence of neurofibrillary pathology such as NFT, NT, and SP dystrophic neurites (DN). DS brains from persons who die in their 30s and early 40s show progressive accumulation of cortical and hippocampal neurofibrillary pathology (Mrak & Griffin, 2004). After age 45, all DS true trisomy cases in the authors' series at the Washington University Alzheimer's Disease Research Center (ADRC)

have typical advanced 'plaque and tangle' AD. Mosaic DS may not be associated with AD pathology at autopsy (Heston, 1984). The dramatic finding of universal histopathology AD in trisomic DS has been confirmed in laboratories throughout the world, thereby providing powerful empirical evidence that accumulation of beta-amyloid, the primary component of SP, drives the neurodegenerative process in AD.

The neuropathology of nonhereditary preclinical AD is characterized by widespread deposition throughout neocortex of preamyloid or diffuse a-beta plaque-like deposits (5.5). Neurofibrillary pathology of dorsolateral cortical areas is sparse or absent. Biochemical analyses may demonstrate increases in soluble and total a-beta protein, and in a-beta dimers, that have not yet formed visible SP. CAA may or may not be present. Presence of the apoE ε4 allele enhances the deposition of CAA (Berg *et al.*, 1998). Hippocampal CA1 and ERC-II pyramidal neurons are well preserved in preclinical AD (Price *et al.*, 2001) (5.6), although quantitative data in this regard on preclinical AD

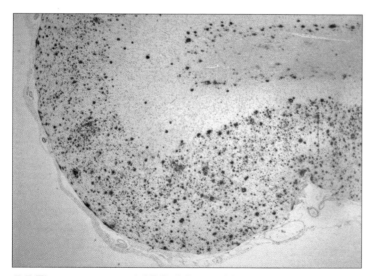

5.5 The neocortex of CDR 0.5 cognitively impaired patients with very mild Alzheimer's disease (Morris *et al.*, 1996) and about 25–40% of nondemented CDR 0 persons (Morris *et al.*, 2004; Petersen, 2004) is widely populated by beta amyloid senile plaques (SP). This prefrontal gyrus has SP filling the outer two-thirds, sparing deep cortical layers 5 and 6, and in the immediately subjacent white matter. Neurofibrillary pathology is usually sparse in this circumstance. (A-beta immunostain with brown substrate, ×1 objective.)

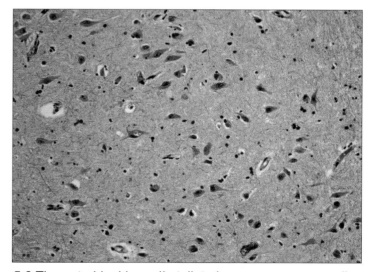

5.6 The entorhinal layer II stellate layer neurons are well preserved and free of tangles in many CDR 0 individuals (Price *et al.*, 2001; Roth, 2001). (Modified Bielschowsky silver method, ×10 objective.)

patients who were well characterized during life are meager.

The hippocampus is affected to a mild or moderate degree in preclinical AD. Braak neurofibrillary lesion severity usually is in stages I–IV, with higher stages V and VI being rare (Morris *et al.*, 2004). Brains with predominately or exclusively preamyloid SP, as originally described by Tagliavini (Tagliavini *et al.*, 1988), may exhibit 'hippocampal sparing' (**5.7**). The hippocampus contains only a few tangles in medial and lateral CA1 and NTs are absent. Granulovacuolar degeneration (GVD) pathology (**5.8**) is sparse in CA1 neurons. Hirano bodies may be present (**5.9**). In striking contrast in such cases, the neocortex may be filled with a-beta deposits that are thioflavine S- and silver-negative.

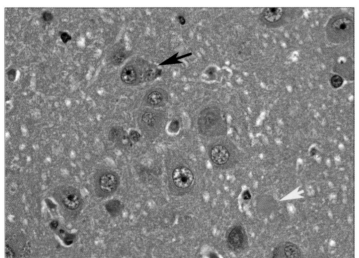

5.7 The hippocampal formation may be spared in a small percentage of persons who have frequent cortical beta amyloid deposits. No senile plaques or neurofibrillary pathology is present. Hippocampal sclerosis, which may account for this 'sparing' pattern, is also absent. (Dual a-beta [red] and PHFtau [black] immunohistochemistry, ×1 objective.)

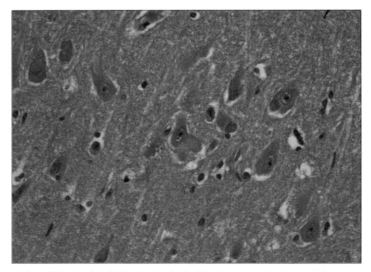

5.8 The hippocampal CA1 region of AD subjects usually exhibits both accentuated granulovacuolar neuronal degeneration (GVD, black arrow) and Hirano bodies, which are structures composed of paracrystalline lattices of actin (yellow arrow). GVD lesions sequester activated caspase-3 (Cotman & Anderson, 1995) and cytoskeletal components such as tubulin. (H&E, ×60 oil objective.)

5.9 A Hirano body is seen in intimate association with a CA1 hippocampal pyramidal neuron. The bodies by EM are enveloped by neuronal plasma membrane. An adjacent pyramidal neuron exhibits cytoplasmic GVD. (H&E, ×20 objective.)

AD pathology in the preclinical pathologic form of the disease is sparse or absent in other brain regions that are typically heavily affected in more advanced AD. For example, the striatum (caudate and putamen) may contain no or only sparse a-beta deposits (never neuritic SP [NSP]) as may scattered subcortical sites (thalamus, hypothalamus) and the cerebellar cortex. Making a firm and confident criteria-based pathologic diagnosis is difficult in preclinical AD cases. These latter cases would not fulfill standard AD pathologic criteria based on lesion burden in the hippocampus, but amply fulfill the original 1985 National Institute on Aging (NIA) quantitative criteria (Khachaturian, 1985) and modified Washington University ADRC criteria derived from them (McKeel et al., 2004). The Consortium to Establish a Registry for Alzheimer's Disease (CERAD) 1991 criteria (Mirra et al., 1991) that depend exclusively on NSP would not be fulfilled by definition. NIA-Reagan Institute criteria as originally formulated (NIA-Reagan Institute Working Group, 1997) apply only to *demented* cases. Similar pathology occurring in CDR 0.5 AD subjects must be assigned a diagnosis of 'low probability AD' under current NIA-Reagan Institute diagnostic guidelines. The authors' group has proposed that preclinical AD cases be classified in the overall AD spectrum as *very mild preclinical AD* (Morris et al., 2004).

Neuropathology of very mild cognitive impairment (MCI)

Morris et al. in 1991 described the neuropathology of persons who died in the earliest clinically detectable stage of evolving dementia, Clinical Dementia Rating 0.5 (CDR 0.5). The neocortical landscape was strikingly similar to the findings described above in brains from persons with preclinical pathologic AD. In 1996, the authors' group characterized the AD pathology found in 9 of 21 brains from presumed nondemented controls studied longitudinally (Morris et al., 1996). The clinical finding that separated the AD (n=9) versus nonAD pathology (n=12) groups in this second study was a history of at least one CDR 0.5 clinical assessment sometime during the patient's course. The neocortex had widespread and massive deposition of predominately diffuse SP (DSP) that stained well with the Hedreen modification of the Bielschowsky silver method and with antibodies to a-beta. Dual Gallyas silver and a-beta immunostaining showed that 97.3% of prefrontal SP were

diffuse (positive for a-beta) and the rest were neuritic as evidenced by their complement of both a-beta and argyrophilic swollen (dystrophic) neurites. Neocortical NFTs and NTs were sparse using both silver and PHFtau immunohistochemistry (IHC). The hippocampal and ERC-II neurofibrillary burden fell in the II–IV Braak staging range (Braak staging was not reported in the paper).

Dr Ronald Peterson's research group at the Mayo Clinic has been instrumental in defining mild cognitive impairment as a clinical entity (Petersen, 2004). They, and others, also recognize that brains of some nondemented persons harbor AD pathology and about 20% of the Mayo series had argyrophilic grain disease (AGD). The authors' nondemented series (Morris et al., 2004) also had a similar high prevalence of AGD (23% of cases with tau-positive and Gallyas-positive limbic grains of Braak) in both the preclinical AD and nonAD groups (DW McKeel, Jr and JL Price, unpublished data).

Neuropathology of mild, moderate, and severe AD

Overview

As AD progresses across the CDR spectrum, the neocortex undergoes a transformation in which: (1) there is an increasing NSP to DSP ratio, (2) NFTs and NTs progressively accumulate, (3) neurons are lost causing progressive disarray of the cortical laminae, (4) cortical synapses are lost, (5) astrocytic glia undergo hypertrophy and hyperplasia (gliosis), and (6) beta-amyloid species accumulate in meningeal arteries and parenchymal capillaries and arteries (CAA). These changes collectively result in cortical and subcortical atrophy that becomes evident at autopsy. The authors' center uses a visual-based scoring system, which was developed by the Washington University ADRC Neuropathology Core, that allows semi-quantitative scores to be assigned rapidly for both external gyral atrophy and ventricular enlargement seen when the brain is sectioned in the coronal plane (*Box 5.3*, overleaf). Hippocampal and entorhinal temporal lobe atrophy is accompanied by varying degrees of both diffuse and lobar atrophy as AD progresses (*Boxes 5.4, 5.5*) (**5.10A, B**, p. 82).

Box 5.3 Scoring brain atrophy at autopsy: the McKeel–Gado visual-based standards approach

McKeel and Gado in 1994 introduced a new method to score external brain atrophy and ventricular dilatation based on a system of visual standards of formalin-fixed autopsy brains from elderly nondemented and demented subjects. Ventricular scoring was assessed on a 1 to 3+ scale at three rostro-caudal levels of the coronally sectioned cerebrum. External gyral atrophy was based on a panel of external photographs of the lateral portions of the cerebral hemisphere. Scores ranged from normal for age or normal (1+) to moderate (2+) or severe (3+).

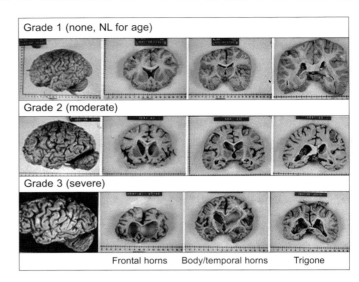

Grade 1 (none, NL for age)

Grade 2 (moderate)

Grade 3 (severe)

Frontal horns   Body/temporal horns   Trigone

Box 5.4 Brain atrophy

Even the healthiest aging is associated with generalized brain atrophy beginning as early as the 4th decade of life and continuing throughout life at annual rate of around 0.4% per year (Fotenos *et al.*, 2005). Brain atrophy likely reflects loss of cortical and subcortical neurons, axonal dropout in the white matter, and shrinkage of large neurons. In these images, age-related brain atrophy is demonstrated by slightly enlarged ventricles and sulcal spaces when comparing axial T1 MRI images (MPRAGE) from a 39-year-old man (**A**) with a nondemented 72-year-old woman (**B**). A number of risk factors in addition to age (Brun & Gustafson, 1976) appear to accelerate the process including hypertension (Gómez-Isla *et al.*, 1996), diabetes (Gómez-Isla *et al.*, 1997), alcohol (Roth, 2001), hyperlipdemia (Cotman & Anderson, 1995), smoking (Horowitz *et al.*, 2004), and homocysteine (Tuszynski *et al.*, 2005).

The presence of AD appears to double the rate of brain atrophy (Brun & Englund, 1981) and pathologic studies suggest cross-sectional and longitudinal estimates of brain atrophy are reflective of neurofibrillary and amyloid plaque burden (Lippa *et al.*, 1992). Accelerated brain atrophy is demonstrated by accentuated sulcal and ventricular spaces in a 75-year-old woman with mild Alzheimer's disease (**C**). In Alzheimer's disease the rate of atrophy is estimated to be about 1% per year. While the presence of brain atrophy is modestly predictive of AD, significant overlap in atrophy pattern between nondemented aging and individuals with AD limit its usefulness in clinical practice as a diagnostic aid.

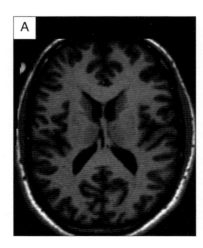
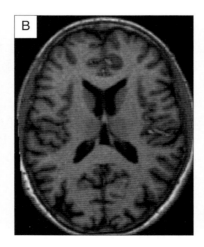
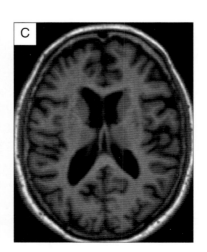

A   B   C

Box 5.5 Hippocampal atrophy

The hippocampus is an important structure in mediating memory processes (Masliah *et al.*, 2001) and is affected early in AD (Nichols *et al.*, 1995). Hippocampal volume loss is considered a valid biomarker of AD neuropathology (Schechter *et al.*, 1981; Lippa *et al.*, 1992). Magnetic resonance- (MR) based volumetric studies are increasingly being employed as surrogate outcome measures of disease with a particular interest in utilizing hippocampal volume changes as endpoints for measuring AD progression in clinical trials (Onoue *et al.*, 2004). Given inherent test-retest variability of behavioral and cognitive measures, sensitive imaging measures of brain aging may prove important in detecting disease associations, exploring mechanisms of brain aging, and allowing more efficient demonstration of an agent's disease modifying effect.

Pathological sections obtained at autopsy demonstrate the hippocampus (arrows) and entorhinal cortex (short arrows) in a nondemented individual (**A**) and an individual with late stage AD (**B**). The temporal horn of the ventricle (arrowhead) is greatly enlarged in the demented individual due to severe atrophy of the entorhinal cortex and the hippocampus. Using MRI, the size and shape of hippocampi can be visualized and quantified in life. The hippocampi of a young male (**C**) and an 86-year-old woman with AD (**D**) are outlined in T1-weighted MRI coronal section (red). The hippocampi of the individual with AD is substantially atrophied as demonstrated by the size and the prominence of the temporal ventricular horns. (MRI images courtesy of D Head and RL Buckner.)

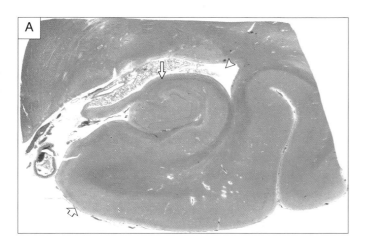
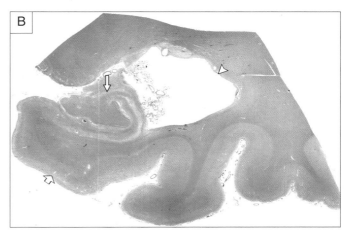
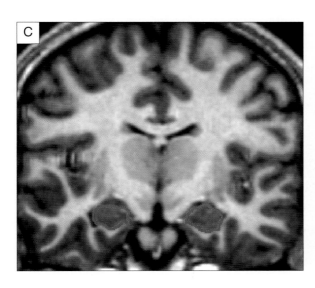
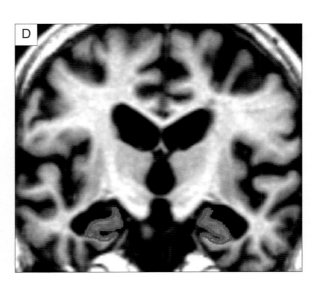

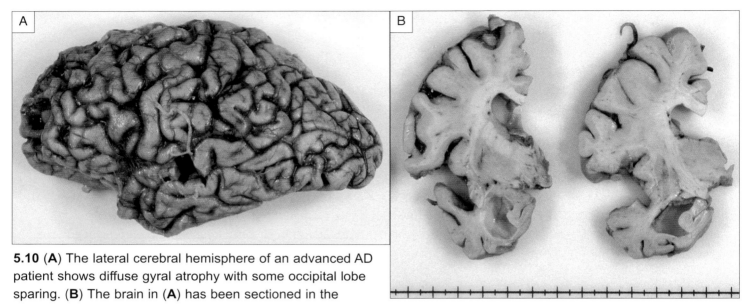

5.10 (A) The lateral cerebral hemisphere of an advanced AD patient shows diffuse gyral atrophy with some occipital lobe sparing. **(B)** The brain in **(A)** has been sectioned in the coronal plane at 1 cm intervals. Sulci are gaping and there is marked atrophy of temporal lobe structures including the gray and white matter, amygdala, and hippocampus. The basal ganglia are relatively spared. The temporal horn of the cerebral ventricular system is widely dilated (3+), and the body is moderately (2+) dilated (see *Box 5.5*). Photographs of the fixed brain at autopsy.

Evolution of plaque subtypes

Most authorities would agree that the proportion of total cortical SP that are neuritic increases during the course of AD. Controversy continues, however, on how this occurs. One possibility is that 'amorphous' preamyloid (a-beta nonargyrophilic thioflavine S-negative) SP gradually condense into more compact but still not fully fibrillar diffuse SP. Ordinary light microscopy, especially when differential interference contrast (DIC) optics or silver methods are used, clearly shows linear structures within DSP (**5.11**). The linear theory of SP evolution then holds that DSP acquire dystrophic neurites that stain with silver and hyperphosphorylated tau antibodies to develop into NSP. A small proportion of NSP then develop central compact beta-amyloid protein cores to become cored NSP.

While the foregoing scenario for SP evolution may be true for certain cortical areas, the generalization that *all* SP go through the same evolutionary process may not be accurate. For example, cerebellar a-beta SP may appear compact and stellate, and even have a central dense core (**5.12A, B**), yet they never develop DNs containing abnormal hyper-phosphorylated tau (PHFtau). Striatal SP lack associated

apoE and remain as DSP throughout the course of AD (Gearing *et al.*, 1997). Medial occipital lobe SP populations have a higher proportion of NSP than DSP at all CDR stages. It is thus clear that local factors in the extracellular tissue milieu, as well as the duration and clinical severity stage of AD, must determine SP morphologic profiles for specific brain regions to a major extent.

Mathematical modeling has been used by several groups to show that SPs are dynamic, porous structures, with SP formation being counterbalanced by SP destruction (Hyman *et al.*, 1993). This is probably mediated by extracellular protease enzymes (Turner *et al.*, 2004). Most recently, Bradley Hyman's group at Harvard Medical School has shown in a series of elegant studies that individual SP tagged with a fluorescent a-beta probe may be observed in a multiphoton microscope over time *in vivo* and their fate can be charted (Christie *et al.*, 2001). Some SP grow (enlarge), some stay the same size over several weeks of observation, and some get smaller in size during the observation period.

5.11 An argyrophilic diffuse senile plaque of a nondemented Down's patient at high optical magnification shows clearly visible internal linear structures that are indicative of a fibrillar substructure. (Modified Bielschowsky method, ×40 objective.)

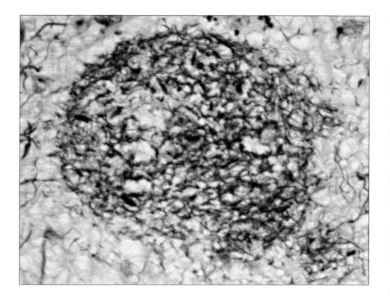

5.12 Cerebellar beta amyloid deposits may have a streak-like morphology (**A**) or be compact and stellate in shape with a central compact core (**B**). Such 'cored' cerebellar plaques never have any tau-positive internal neuritic staining. (A-beta immunohistochemistry with a brown substrate. **A**: ×10 objective; **B**: ×20 objective.)

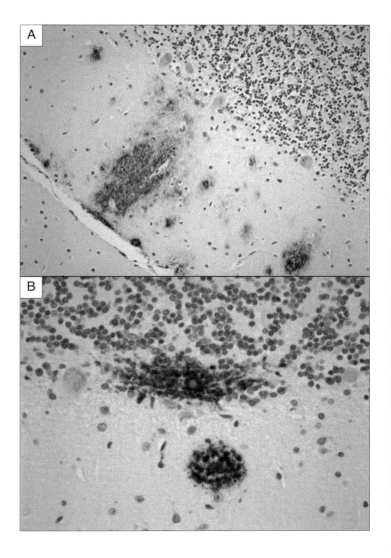

Progression of neurofibrillary pathology

Neurofibrillary pathology (NFP) lesions progressively accumulate, in a hierarchical manner embodied in the Braak staging scheme (Braak & Braak, 1991), in the neocortex of clearly demented AD subjects. Most mild, moderate, and advanced dementia severity AD patients have Braak stage IV–VI brain pathology by the time they die. Perhaps most dramatic is the build-up of aggregated insoluble tau in neuronal processes – axons and dendrites – as NT (**5.13**). At first this process is focal in deeper cortical laminae (V, especially). Cortical layer III then becomes involved so that two 'bands' of tau-positive tangles and NTs appear at low power (**5.14**). Transcortical NT deposition is the rule in persons who die at CDR 3. It is surprising that combined NFP may occupy up to 30% of the cortical ribbon area (DW McKeel, Jr, unpublished observations).

Neuritic plaque PHFtau-positive neurites are a major component of NFP that build up in neocortex in concert with NFT and NT (**5.15A–D**). SP neurites, at various stages of SP evolution, may contain different insoluble protein markers. The a-beta precursor APP is an early marker (Cras *et al.*, 1991), ubiquitin is an intermediate stage marker (He *et al.*, 1993), and PHFtau is a relatively late marker of NSP.

Hippocampal CA1 fields, the subiculum, ERC, and transitional allocortex also accumulate NFT, NT, and NSP during the course of AD (**5.16**). Initially, DSP are progressively replaced by NSP in the outer molecular layer of the dentate fascia, the terminal field of the perforant pathway (**5.17**). Pretangles, best seen in PHFtau or certain silver preparations, harbor granular tau that forms a distinct perinuclear ring (**5.18**). In late stage AD (CDR 3), even the so-called 'silent zone' of the parasubiculum and the clouds of amorphous a-beta protein in the presubiculum accumulate NFT and NT. There is a dramatic replacement of intraneuronal tangles by extracellular ('ghost' or 'tombstone') tangles in both CA1 and ERC-II as AD evolves into the last stages (**5.19**).

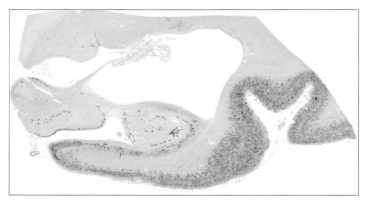

5.13 A typical medial temporal lobe section used for Braak staging of an advanced AD patient brain shows widespread red plaques throughout CA1, dentate fascia, subiculum compartments, entorhinal cortex (ERC), transitional allocortex, and temporal isocortex. Contrasting black neurofibrillary tangles and neuropil threads form a single black band in CA1-subiculum and ERC, then diverge into two distinct bands in allocortex and isocortex. This pattern would be indicative of at least Braak stage IV (Braak & Braak, 1991). Final staging would require examination of the occipital cortex in a preparation such as the one depicted in **5.14** in order to define the total extent of neocortical neurofibrillary pathology. (Dual a-beta [red] and PHFtau [black] immunostain, ×1 objective.)

5.14 PHFtau (PHF-1 tau antibody, gift of Peter Davies) defines two layers of advanced Alzheimer's disease neocortical neurofibrillary pathology. Insoluble tau deposition at this stage (Braak V or VI) is transcortical when viewed at high magnification (see **5.16**). (PHFtau immunohistochemistry with brown substrate, ×1 objective.)

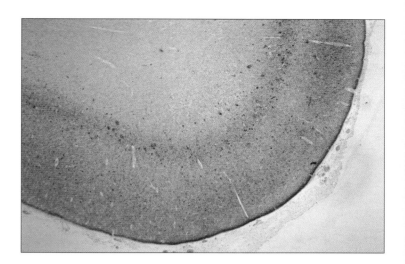

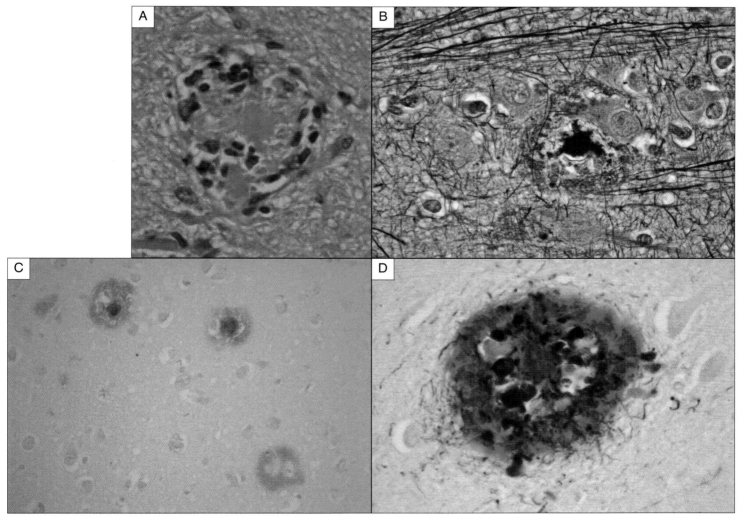

5.15 (A) A neuritic cored senile plaque is surrounded by astrocytes (oval nuclei) and microglia (elongate nuclei). (H&E, ×40 objective.) **(B)** Another cored neuritic plaque stained with modified Bielschowsky silver shows enhanced silver affinity of the compact central amyloid core. (×40 objective.) **(C)** Preamyloid a-beta plaques lack tau neurites but may have central compact amyloid cores (upper right and center plaques). (Dual a-beta [red] and PHFtau [black] immunohistochemistry, 40x objective.) **(D)** A 'mature' cored neuritic plaque contains internal swollen dystrophic neurites that label strongly with PHFtau (black bulbous structures) that contrasts with the red beta amyloid. Note numerous tau-positive neurites at the plaque periphery. (Dual a-beta [red] and PHFtau [black] immunohistochemistry, ×40 objective.)

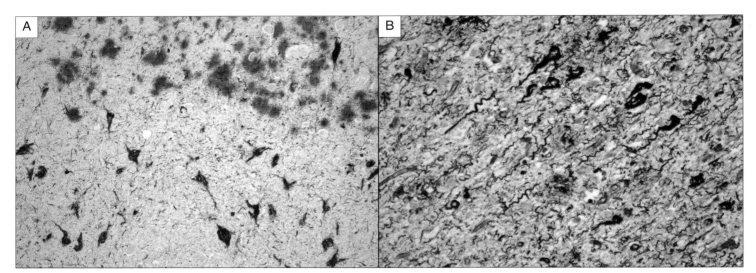

5.16 (A) Outer entorhinal cortex in advanced AD shows most stellate layer II neurons to have either internal or ghost (extracellular) tau-positive neurofibrillary tangles (larger discreet black structures). Note that some ghost tangles label with a-beta antibody (red substrate), a phenomenon that several laboratories have previously reported. In addition, the entire area is suffused with a myriad of neuropil threads containing aggregated insoluble tau. Numerous red a-beta plaques are evident in the lower cortical laminae. (Dual a-beta [red] and PHFtau [black] immunohistochemistry, ×40 objective.) **(B)** A Gallyas silver preparation of the same brain region shown in panel **(A)** dramatically highlights contorted neuropil threads, tangles and corkscrew-like dendritic processes of entorhinal pyramidal neurons. (Gallyas silver method, ×40 objective.)

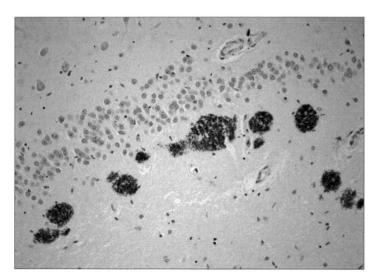

5.17 A row of senile plaques accumulates in advanced AD at the terminal fields of the perforant pathway (PP) within the molecular layer of the dentate fascia of the hippocampal formation. This region is rich in PP synapses that represent the ends of layer II entorhinal cortex stellate neurons. (A-beta amyloid preparation with brown substrate, ×10 objective.)

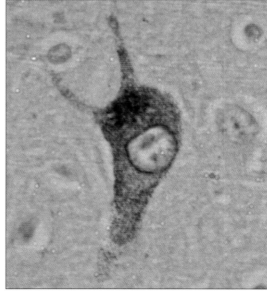

5.18 Pretangles are an early stage in the development of mature intraneuronal neurofibrillary tangles (NFT). The PHF tau appear more punctate than the condensed fascicles of tau in mature intraneuronal tangles. In addition, there is often a clearly visible perinuclear ring of condensed tau, a so-called 'perinuclear net'. (PHF tau immunohistochemistry, ×40 objective.)

5.19 The Gallyas silver method is excellent for displaying the loose internal structure of ghost tangles that have been partly digested by extracellular proteases. The neuronal cell body has disappeared. Thus, these structures are often referred to as 'tombstone' tangles. They are particularly common in the outer entorhinal cortex (shown here) and in the CA1 region of the hippocampal formation. (Gallyas silver method, ×40 objective.)

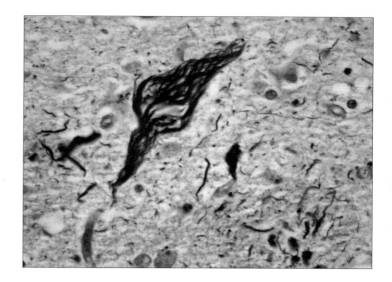

Neuronal dysfunction and death

Alterations in neuronal function are undoubtedly a fundamental cause of cognitive impairment and dementia in AD. Functional magnetic resonance imaging (fMRI), MRI spectroscopy, SPECT (single photon emission computed tomography) and positron emission tomography (PET) neuroimaging studies indicate different initial sites of neuronal dysmetabolism (posterior parietal, posterior cingulate) than anatomic studies have generally shown. With but a few previous exceptions (Brun and Gustafson, 1976; Brun and Englund, 1981), more recent histopathologic studies have not shown the initial sites of neuronal and synaptic losses to occur in the posterior parietal and cingulate regions. This striking discrepancy between study modalities needs to be resolved by additional research.

Histopathologic methods including unbiased stereology have shown that certain classes of neurons are lost at different rates during the course of AD. The reasons behind this exquisite *neuronal vulnerability* are surprisingly not well understood. Why, for example, do 60% of ERC-II stellate neurons that give rise to the perforant pathway die by CDR

0.5 (Gómez-Isla *et al.*, 1996)? In contrast, the population of large pyramidal neurons in the superior temporal sulcus are maintained until the late CDR stages (Gómez-Isla *et al.*, 1997).

While the apoptotic cascade has been widely implicated as the primary cause of neuronal death in AD, a substantive body of research indicates that parts of this pathway are by-passed (Cotman & Anderson, 1995; Roth, 2001). Activated caspase-3 has been localized to GVD lesions in hippocampal CA1 pyramidal neurons. Caspase-6 has recently been proposed as a molecular link whereby cytoplasmic subcellular a-beta dimers may trigger changes in tau that lead to paired helical filament and tangle formation (Horowitz *et al.*, 2004*)*. An absolute or relative lack of key growth factors (Tuszynski *et al.*, 2005) or trans-synaptic degeneration may also contribute to selective neuronal death in AD. Together these neuronal death mechanisms combine to cause progressive disarray of the cortical laminae and white matter (axon loss, *Box 5.6*) (**5.20**) at the microscopic level (Brun & Gustafson, 1976; Brun & Englund, 1981).

Box 5.6 White matter lesions

Abnormalities are commonly found in the cerebral white matter in AD and nondemented aging. These white matter lesions (WMLs) are hyperintense on T2 images with corresponding low intensity on T1 images, as seen in an 88-year-old man with mild AD (**A**). For comparison, normal white matter is present in a 76-year-old man with AD (**B**). WMLs are consistently associated with age, hypertension, and other cardiovascular risk factors (Olichney et al., 2000) and are thus commonly considered part of the spectrum of vascular-related injury (Nicoll et al., 2004). In nondemented individuals, WMLs are associated with reduced processing speed, memory, and executive function in nondemented individuals (Nochlin et al., 1998). The clinical significance of WMLs in AD remains less clear. Pathologic studies suggest that individuals with more WMLs have a higher risk of developing AD (Houlden et al., 2000; Bertram & Tanzi, 2004) and require less neuropathologic AD burden to demonstrate cognitive impairment (Lippa et al., 1998) and dementia (Snowdon et al., 1997) than individuals without these lesions. Additionally, radiological studies suggest individuals in the earliest clinical stages of AD may be more vulnerable to the clinically-relevant cognitive influence of WML than nondemented individuals with similar WML burden (Burns et al., 2005).

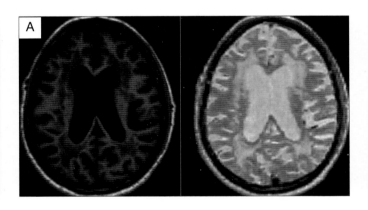

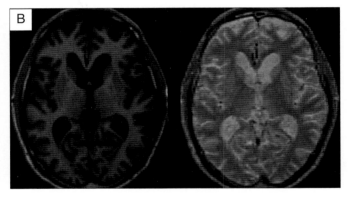

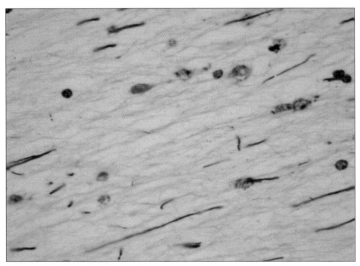

5.20 Cortical white matter shows severe axon and myelin loss in cases of AD that have remained at CDR 3 for prolonged periods. This modified Bielschowsky silver preparation shows marked axon loss of the deep centrum semiovale in an advanced AD brain. (Modified Bielschowsky silver method, ×40 objective.)

Loss of cortical and hippocampal synapses

The strongest correlation with dementia severity that the authors' research has identified is a correlation of $r^2=0.85$ between CDR at death and the total number of hippocampal synaptophysin-immunoreactive synapses, measured individually by unbiased stereology at ×3,200, in the terminal field of the perforant pathway (NS Havlioglu and DW McKeel, Jr, unpublished data). Approximately 80% of outer molecular layer synapses of the dentate fascia are axon endings of ERC-II stellate neurons (Lippa et al., 1992). Neocortical synapses are also progressively lost during the course of AD. Masliah in collaboration with the authors' group demonstrated loss of prefrontal cortex synaptophysin activity using a dot blot assay in brain homogenates from CDR 0.5 AD individuals (Masliah et al., 2001). Progressive loss of the same marker was shown in the higher CDR groups. Many other laboratories have amply confirmed these findings of profound synaptic loss as a major cause of dementia in general, not just as a key mechanism in AD.

Astrocytic 'gliosis'

Transcription of a major marker of astrocytic glia, the intermediate filament glial fibrillary acidic protein (GFAP), is strongly upregulated during normal aging (Schechter *et al.*, 1981; Nichols *et al.*, 1995). In AD, cortical and hippocampal astrocytes undergo hypertrophy and hyperplasia, a process pathologists refer to as 'gliosis'. Gliosis under the microscope may reflect primarily the enlargement of the astrocyte cell body and processes rather than an actual proliferation of this major glial class (**5.21**). Quantitative image analysis has shown a strong linear and reciprocal increase in cortical glia (primarily astrocytes) at sites where neurons degenerate and are lost (Schechter *et al.*, 1981) (**5.21**).

Cerebral (a-beta) amyloid angiopathy

'Congophilic' amyloid angiopathy was an early name given to this lesion in which beta-pleated sheets of beta-amyloid peptides accumulate in meningeal arteries and parenchymal capillaries and arteries (but rarely in veins) (**5.22A, B**). The dye, Congo red, intercalates into the beta-pleated sheet and exhibits circular dichroism and 'apple green' birefringence under polarized light. Electron microscopy (EM) shows 10 nm twisted filaments. Many proteins as widely diverse as transthyretin and hormones such as glucagon undergo similar physicochemical transformation to form amyloid fibrils *in vivo* or *in vitro* (Onoue *et al.*, 2004). Also, as early as the 1920s, Paul Divry (Attems & Jellinger, 2004) recognized that amyloid proteins may accumulate not only

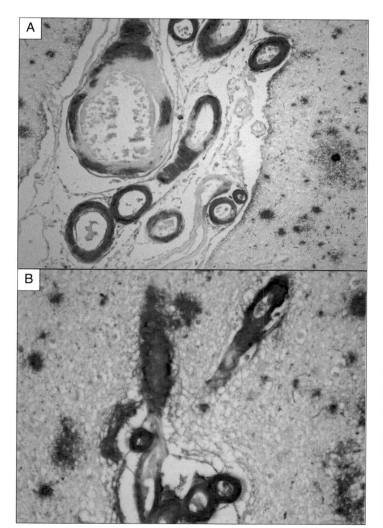

5.21 The anterior cingulate cortex of an advanced AD patient shows marked neuron loss with replacement gliosis (Brun & Gustafson, 1976; Gómez-Isla *et al.*, 1996; Onoue *et al.*, 2004). The hypertrophied astrocytes have flame-red stellate processes and more cytoplasm than is usually evident in normal brains. (H&E, ×20 objective.)

5.22 (A) Beta amyloid deposition (or formation) is common in the leptomeningeal arterial system in AD. Amyloid-laden blood vessels often have 'double lumens' by H&E. This is a florid example. Note amyloid plaques and tangles in the adjacent brain. (Dual a-beta [red] and PHFtau [black] immunohistochemistry, ×10 objective.) **(B)** Internal and penetrating parenchymal arteries in neocortex may also harbor beta amyloid deposits in AD. (Dual a-beta [red] and PHFtau [black] immunohistochemistry, ×20 objective.)

in arteries but in cerebral capillaries, a lesion he referred to as 'dyshoria'. Divry was apparently struck by the spike-like protrusions extending from the capillary wall into brain parenchyma (**5.23**) and was moved to speculate whether the spikes represented proteinaceous ingress into or egress from the brain. The issue has not been completely settled by recent research.

During the last half of the 20th century three additional methods (described, illustrated, and referenced in Chapter 3) were developed to demonstrate CAA effectively: the Gallyas silver method, thioflavine S and T fluorescent dyes, and immunostaining with a-beta protein antibodies. Although a-beta 1–40 has been identified as a major component of most cases of AD-related CAA, other molecules including a-beta 1–42 and cystatin C may be co-deposited or be the sole cause of CAA (Revesz *et al.*, 2003).

CAA may occur as part of AD or as an isolated lesion in the healthy aging brain. Recent neurosurgical series of operated lobar hemorrhages in elderly persons disclose a high prevalence of CAA that is often thought to be the causative lesion for bleeding (Izumihara *et al.*, 2005). CAA burden in the brain is exacerbated by the presence of one or two apoE ε4 alleles (Olichney *et al.*, 2000).

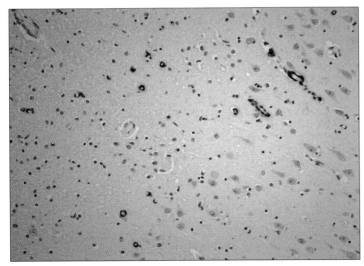

5.23 Capillaries may also become laden with beta-amyloid, especially in medial occipital visual cortex. This example is from entorhinal cortex, a less commonly involved area. Spike-like protrusions of amyloid from brain capillaries have been referred to as 'dyshoric' amyloid angiopathy (e.g. Nicoll *et al.*, 2004; Izumihara *et al.*, 2005). (A-beta immunohistochemistry with brown substrate, ×10 objective.)

The clinically important question is the role that CAA plays in causing or contributing to dementia severity. There is suggestive evidence from series of patients with hereditary CAA syndromes (Dutch, Icelandic, British) that a subset of these patients become demented in the absence of significant AD plaque and tangle pathology (Nicoll *et al.*, 2004). Ultimately this is a difficult question to answer based on current evidence. Assessing mild cognitive impairment and ruling out, for example, preamyloid deposits and early forms of tangles ('pretangles') requires rigorous methodology that has not always been applied to the series mentioned above. Although admittedly subject to challenge, it is the author's belief that CAA can cause progressive cognitive impairment as the sole or dominant dementing pathology.

Comparing sporadic and familial AD

The pathology of DS trisomy 21, a form of genetically determined dementia, has already been described in this chapter. Similar to many pedigrees with a mutation in APP, PS1 or PS2, DS cerebral pathology and dementia appear decades before similar clinical and pathologic changes do in brains of sporadic AD patients. Some PS1 mutations (Nochlin *et al.*, 1998) lead to unusually severe CAA. 'Cotton wool plaques' are another lesion that has been recently described in brains of persons with PS1 mutations (Houlden *et al.*, 2000). A worldwide intensive search is underway to define additional risk factors besides the apoE ε4 allele and APP or presenilin gene mutations that determine the variable age of onset in very early onset (before age 40), early onset (before age 65) and late onset sporadic and FAD (Bertram & Tanzi, 2004).

Another intriguing aspect of FAD pathology is the higher than expected prevalence of co-occurring Lewy body disease. Lippa *et al.* (1998), for example, found that a majority of FAD brains harbored Lewy bodies demonstrable with alpha-synuclein immunohistochemistry (IHC) in the amygdala. The authors have studied a small pedigree in which three members from two generations had autosomal dominant AD with onset in their 20s and death 10–20 years later. One brain from a 43-year-old affected woman who survived 19 years weighed only 700 g and exhibited global knife edge gyral atrophy and severe diffuse ventricular enlargement (**5.24A, B**) at autopsy. The neocortex and hippocampus showed typical severe AD plaque and tangle with CAA pathology (**5.25**).

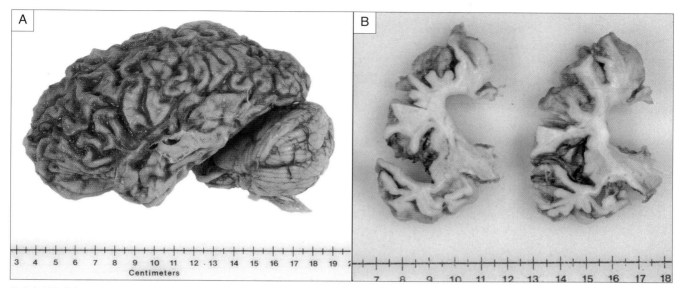

5.24 (**A**) A lateral view of the formalin-fixed 700 g brain at autopsy from a 43-year-old woman with familial AD who survived 19 years. Note the striking overall size decrease of the cerebrum compared to the cerebellum. Also noted the marked sulcal narrowing that involves all four major lobes and approaches a 'knife-edge' appearance focally. (**B**) The same brain after being sectioned at 1 cm intervals in the coronal plane. All portions are severely affected including the deep white matter, basal ganglia, and hippocampal formation. Autopsy fixed brain specimen.

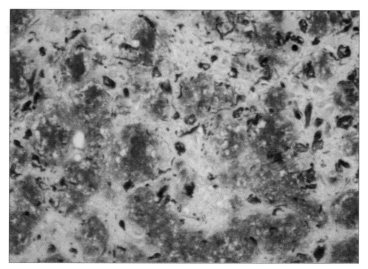

5.25 Microscopically, the brain shown in **5.24** and **5.26** revealed florid deposition of beta-amyloid and the full extent of tau-positive neurofibrillary pathology. This section of the subicular complex has numerous confluent amyloid plaques (red) and tangles (black). (Dual a-beta [red] and PHFtau [black] immunohistochemistry, ×20 objective.)

Abundant Lewy pathology in the form of classical Lewy bodies (substantia nigra), Lewy neurites that occurred diffusely and concentrated in the hippocampal CA1/2 (sometimes referred to as CA2/3) junction, and cortical Lewy bodies, was detected throughout brainstem, limbic structures (including the amygdala), and neocortical areas using alpha-synuclein IHC (**5.26A, B**).

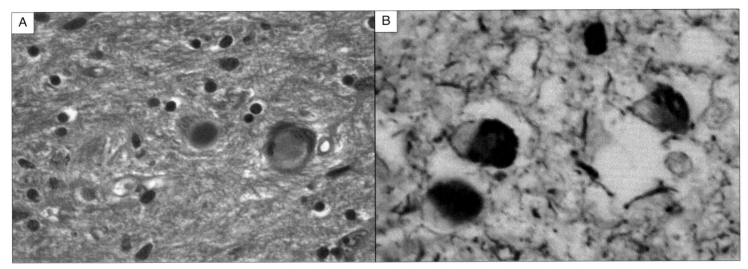

5.26 (**A**) The mid-brain substantia nigra of the familial AD case depicted in **5.24** and **5.25** also showed classical Lewy bodies. Note the basophilic darker center and the clear halo that separates the filamentous inclusion from the surrounding cell cytoplasm. Oligodendrocytes and a small arteriole with red blood cells (7 μm diameter) in the lumen may be used for size comparisons). (H&E stain, ×40 objective.) (**B**) The same brain also revealed widespread limbic (not shown) and neocortical Lewy bodies (CLBs). Four clustered CLBs in superior temporal cortex are strongly labeled with alpha-synuclein (aSYN) antibody LB-509. Lewy neurites that are also aSYN positive are present in the adjacent neuropil. (Alpha synuclein immunohistochemistry, ×40 objective.)

References

American Academy of Neurology/Quality Standards Subcommittee (1994). Practice parameter for diagnosis and evaluation of dementia. *Neurology* 44:2203–2206.

Arai T, Ikeda K, Akiyama H, *et al.* (1999). A high incidence of apolipoprotein E epsilon 4 allele in middle-aged non-demented subjects with cerebral amyloid beta protein deposits. *Acta Neuropathol.* 97(1):82–84.

Attems J, Jellinger KA (2004). Only cerebral capillary amyloid angiopathy correlates with Alzheimer pathology – a pilot study. *Acta Neuropathol.* 107(2):83–90.

Berg L, McKeel DW Jr, Miller JP, *et al.* (1998). Clinicopathologic studies in cognitively healthy aging and Alzheimer disease: relation of histologic markers to dementia severity, age, sex, and apolipoprotein E genotype. *Arch. Neurol.* 55(3):326–335.

Bertram L, Tanzi RE (2004). The current status of Alzheimer's disease genetics: what do we tell the patients? (Review) (83 refs). *Pharmacol. Res.* 50(4):385–396.

Braak H, Braak E (1991). The neuropathologic stageing of Alzheimer-related changes. *Acta Neuropathol. (Berlin)* 82:239–259.

Brun A, Englund E (1976). Regional pattern of degeneration in Alzheimer's disease: neuronal loss and histopathological grading. *Histopathology* 5:459–464.

Brun A, Gustafson L (1976). Distribution of cerebral degeneration in Alzheimer's disease. A clinico-pathological study. *Archiv fur Psychiatrie und Nervenkrankheiten* 223(1):15–33.

Burns JM, Church JA, Johnson DK, *et al.* (2005). White matter lesions are prevalent but differentially related with cognition in aging and early Alzheimer's disease. *Arch. Neurol.* 62:1870–1876.

Christie RH, Bacskai BJ, Zipfel WR, *et al.* (2001). Growth arrest of individual senile plaques in a model of Alzheimer's disease observed by *in vivo* multiphoton microscopy. *J. Neurosci.* **21**(3):858–864.

Chui H, Zhang Q (1997). Evaluation of dementia: a systematic study of the usefulness of the American Academy of Neurology's practice parameters. *Neurology* **49**:925–935.

Clarfield AM (1988). The reversible dementias: do they reverse? *Ann. Intern. Med.* **109**:476–486.

Cotman CW, Anderson AJ (1995). A potential role for apoptosis in neurodegeneration and Alzheimer's disease. *Mol. Neurobiol.* **10**:19–45.

Cras P, Kawai M, Lowery D, *et al.* (1991). Senile plaque neurites in Alzheimer disease accumulate amyloid precursor protein. *Proc. Nat. Acad. Sci. USA* **88**(17):7552–7556.

Ebly EM, Parhad IM, Hogan DB, *et al.* (1994). Prevalence and types of dementia in the very old: results from the Canadian Study of Health and Aging. *Neurology* **44**(9):1593–1600.

Fotenos AF, Snyder AZ, Girton LE, *et al.* (2005). Normative estimates of cross-sectional and longitudinal brain volume decline in aging and AD. *Neurology* **64**:1032–1039.

Gearing M, Levey AI, Mirra SS (1997). Diffuse plaques in the striatum in Alzheimer disease (AD): relationship to the striatal mosaic and selected neuropeptide markers. *J. Neuropathol. Exp. Neurol.* **56**:1363–1370.

Gómez-Isla T, Hollister R, West H, *et al.* (1997). Neuronal loss correlates with but exceeds neurofibrillary tangles in Alzheimer's disease. *Ann. Neurol.* **41**:17–24.

Gómez-Isla T, Price JL, McKeel DW Jr, *et al.* (1996). Profound loss of layer II entorhinal cortex neurons in very mild Alzheimer's disease. *J. Neurosci.* **16**:4491–4500.

He Y, Delaere P, Duyckaerts C, *et al.* (1993). Two distinct ubiquitin immunoreactive senile plaques in Alzheimer's disease: relationship with the intellectual status in 29 cases. *Acta Neuropathol.* **86**(1):109–116.

Hebert LE, Beckett LA, Scherr PA, *et al.* (2001). Annual incidence of Alzheimer disease in the United States projected to the years 2000 through 2050. *Alz. Dis. Assoc. Dis.* **15**(4):169–173.

Heston LL (1984). Down's syndrome and Alzheimer's dementia: defining an association. (Review) (15 refs) *Psych. Develop.* **2**:287–294.

Horowitz PM, Patterson KR, Guillozet-Bongaarts AL, *et al.* (2004). Early N-terminal changes and caspase-6 cleavage of tau in Alzheimer's disease. *J. Neurosci.* **24**(36):7895–7902.

Houlden H, Baker M, McGowan E, *et al.* (2000). Variant Alzheimer's disease with spastic paraparesis and cotton wool plaques is caused by PS1 mutations that lead to exceptionally high amyloid-b concentrations. *Ann. Neurol.* **48**:806–808.

Hyman BT, Marzloff K, Arriagada PV (1993). The lack of accumulation of senile plaques or amyloid burden in Alzheimer's disease suggests a dynamic balance between amyloid deposition and resolution. *J. Neuropathol. Exp. Neurol.* **52**(6):594–600.

Izumihara A, Suzuki M, Ishihara T (2005). Recurrence and extension of lobar hemorrhage related to cerebral amyloid angiopathy: multivariate analysis of clinical risk factors. *Surg. Neurol.* **64**(2):160–164.

Khachaturian ZS (1985). Diagnosis of Alzheimer's disease. *Arch. Neurol.* **42**:1097–1105.

Knopman DS, DeKosky ST, Cummings JL, *et al.* (2001). Practice parameter: diagnosis of dementia (an evidence-based review). Report of the Quality Standards Subcommittee of the American Academy of Neurology. *Neurology* **56**:1143–1153.

Lippa CF, Fujiwara H, Mann DM, *et al.* (1998). Lewy bodies contain altered alpha-synuclein in brains of many familial Alzheimer's disease patients with mutations in presenilin and amyloid precursor protein genes. *Am. J. Pathol.* **153**(5):1365–1370.

Lippa CF, Hamos JE, Pulaski-Salo D, *et al.* (1992). Alzheimer's disease and aging: effects on perforant pathway perikarya and synapses. *Neurobiol. Aging* **13**(3):405–411.

Masliah E, Mallory M, Alford M, *et al.* (2001). Altered expression of synaptic proteins occurs early during progression of Alzheimer's disease. *Neurology* **56**:127–129.

McKeel DW Jr, Price JL, Miller JP, *et al.* (2004). Neuropathologic criteria for diagnosing Alzheimer Disease in persons with pure dementia of Alzheimer type. *J. Neuropathol. Exp. Neurol.* **63**:1028–1037.

McKhann G, Drachman D, Folstein M, *et al.* (1984). Clinical diagnosis of Alzheimer's disease: report of the NINCDS-ADRDA Work Group under the auspices of Department of Health and Human Services Task Force on Alzheimer's disease. *Neurology* **34**·939–944.

Mendez MF, Cummings JL (2003). Alzheimer's Disease. In: *Dementia: A Clinical Approach*. 3rd edn. Butterworth Heinemann, Philadelphia, pp. 67–95.

Mintun MA, LaRossa GN, Sheline YI, *et al.* (2006). ["C]PIB in a nondemented polulation: potential antecedent marker of Alzheimer's disease. *Neurology* 67:446–452.

Mirra SS, Heyman A, McKeel D Jr, *et al.* (1991). The Consortium to Establish a Registry for Alzheimer's Disease (CERAD). Part II. Standardization of the neuropathologic assessment of Alzheimer's disease. *Neurology* **41**:479–486.

Morris JC, McKeel DW Jr, Buckles VD, *et al.* (2004). Neuropathological markers of preclinical Alzheimer's disease in nondemented aging. *J. Neurosci. Abstr.* **902** online (URL: http://sfn.scholarone.com/itin2004/index.html).

Morris JC, McKeel DW Jr, Storandt M, *et al.* (1991). Very mild Alzheimer's disease: informant-based clinical, psychometric, and pathological distinction from normal aging. *Neurology* **41**:469–478.

Morris JC, Storandt M, McKeel DW Jr, *et al.* (1996). Cerebral amyloid deposition and diffuse plaques in 'normal' aging: evidence for presymptomatic and very mild Alzheimer's disease. *Neurology* **46**:707–729.

Mrak RE, Griffin WS (2004). Trisomy 21 and the brain. (Review) (78 refs) *J. Neuropathol. Exp. Neurol.* **63**(7):679–685.

NIA-Reagan Institute Working Group consensus recommendations for the postmortem diagnosis of Alzheimer's disease (1997). The National Institute on Aging, and Reagan Institute Working Group on Diagnostic Criteria for Neuropathological Assessment of Alzheimer's disease. *Neurobiol. Aging* **18**(4 Suppl):S1–S2.

Nichols NR, Finch CE, Nelson JF (1995). Food restriction delays the age-related increase in GFAP mRNA in rat hypothalamus. *Neurobiol. Aging* **16**(1):105–110.

Nicoll JA, Yamada M, Frackowiak J, *et al.* (2004). Cerebral amyloid angiopathy plays a direct role in the pathogenesis of Alzheimer's disease. Pro-CAA position statement. (Review) (61 refs). *Neurobiol. Aging* **25**(5):589–597; discussion 603–604.

Nochlin D, Bird TD, Nemens EJ, *et al.* (1998). Amyloid angiopathy in a Volga German family with Alzheimer's disease and a presenilin-2 mutation (N141I). (Case Reports.) *Ann. Neurol.* **43**:131–135.

Olichney JM, Hansen LA, Lee JH, *et al.* (2000). Relationship between severe amyloid angiopathy, apolipoprotein E genotype, and vascular lesions in Alzheimer's disease. (Review) (31 refs). *Annals NY Acad. Sci.* **903**:138–143.

Onoue S, Ohshima K, Debari K, *et al.* (2004). Mishandling of the therapeutic peptide glucagon generates cytotoxic amyloidogenic fibrils. *Pharm. Res.* **21**(7):1274–1283.

Petersen RC (2004). Mild cognitive impairment as a diagnostic entity. (Review) (50 refs) *J. Int. Med.* **256**(3):183–194.

Price JL, Ko AI, Wade MJ, *et al.* (2001). Neuron number in entorhinal cortex and CA1 in preclinical Alzheimer's disease. *Arch. Neurol.* **58**:1395–1402.

Reisberg B, Ferris SH, de Leon MJ, *et al.* (1982). Global Deterioration Scale. *Am. J. Psych.* **139**:1136–1139.

Revesz T, Ghiso J, Lashley T, *et al.* (2003). Cerebral amyloid angiopathies: a pathologic, biochemical, and genetic view. (Review) (80 refs). *J. Neuropathol. Exp. Neurol.* **62**:885–898.

Roth KA (2001). Caspases, apoptosis, and Alzheimer disease: causation, correlation, and confusion. (Review) (84 refs). *J. Neuropathol. Exp. Neurol.* **60**(9):829–838.

Sano M (2004). A guide to diagnosis of Alzheimer's disease. *CNS Spectrums* **9**(7 Suppl 5):16–19.

Schechter R, Yen SH, Terry RD (1981). Fibrous astrocytes in senile dementia of the Alzheimer type. *J. Neuropathol. Exp. Neurol.* **40**(2):95–101.

Small GW, Rabins PV, Barry PP, *et al.* (1997). Diagnosis and treatment of Alzheimer disease and related disorders. Consensus statement of the American Association for Geriatric Psychiatry, the Alzheimer's Association, and the American Geriatrics Society. *JAMA* **278**:1363–1371.

Snowdon DA, Greiner LH, Mortimer JA, *et al.* (1997). Brain infarction and the clinical expression of Alzheimer disease. *JAMA* **277**:813–817.

Tagliavini F, Giaccone G, Frangione B, *et al.* (1988). Preamyloid deposits in the cerebral cortex of patients with Alzheimer's disease and nondemented individuals. *Neurosci. Lett.* **93**(2–3):191–196.

Turner AJ, Fisk L, Nalivaeva NN (2004). Targeting amyloid-degrading enzymes as therapeutic strategies in neurodegeneration. *Ann. NY Acad. Sci.* **1035**:1–20.

Tuszynski MH, Thal L, Pay M, *et al.* (2005). A phase 1 clinical trial of nerve growth factor gene therapy for Alzheimer disease. *Nature Medicine* **11**(5):551–555.

Appendix

ADRC Washington University School of Medicine: Bielschowsky-MBT (for tangles)

20% silver nitrate
20 g silver nitrate add to
100 ml DH2O, stir to dissolve

Ammoniacal silver
Add vacuumed ammonia to 20% silver drop by drop until the solution gets cloudy then turns clear, filter before use

5% Hypo
5 g sodium thiosulfate
100 ml DH2O mix and dissolve

Developer
100 ml DH2O
20 ml 35% formaldehyde
0.5 g citric acid
1 drop nitric acid, mix and dissolve in order

1 Hydrate slides to DH2O and rinse for 5 minutes.
2 Impregnate slides in 20% silver nitrate for 20 minutes at room temperature.
3 Rinse in DH2O approximately 5 minutes.
4 Pour the ammonical silver solution (filtered) on the slides and let it sit for 15 minutes.
5 Pour the ammonical silver solution into a clean container; wash the slides in a weak ammonia solution for 3–5 minutes.
6 Add 3 drops of developer per 100 ml silver solution. Stir.
7 Pour off the wash solution and pour on the developer solution. Developing takes 5–10 minutes (watch carefully).
8 Rinse in DH2O for about 5 minutes.
9 Place in hypo solution for 30 seconds to 3 minutes; watch until it turns a nice brown color.
10 Rinse in DH2O for 3–5 minutes, then dehydrate back to xylene, coverslip.

Notes
1 *Always* acid clean your dishes.
2 *Never* use metal in silver solutions.
3 *Always* wear gloves when using silver – it will develop on your skin.
4 *Always* use fresh reagents.
5 Use powder-free gloves only.
6 Place ammonia on vacuum for 20 minutes.

Materials needed
1 Silver nitrate – EMS #21052
2 Sodium thiosulfate – Fisher #AC20287-5000
3 Citric acid – Sigma C7129

ADRC Washington University School of Medicine: hematoxylin and eosin (H&E)

1 Run the slide down to DH2O.
2 Place in hematoxylin for 10 minutes.
3 Rinse in DH2O for 5 minutes, 1 dip in acid alcohol, wash in DH2O, 8 dips in ammonia water, wash in DH2O for 15 minutes.
4 Dip 1–3 times in 95% alcohol.
5 Place in eosin for 3 minutes.
6 Wash in DH2O for 3–5 minutes.
7 Quickly run down to xylene and coverslip.

Notes
1 Use the ThermoShandon Instant Hematoxylin and Eosin with phyloxine for this stain protocol (2/13/02) order #6765015.
2 Follow the protocol in the AFIP *Staining Manual* to make eosin with phyloxine.

National Alzheimer's Coordinating Center (NACC)

Headquarters: University of Washington, Seattle.

Principal Investigator: Walter A Kukull, PhD Epidemiology, University of Washington.

Funding source: National Institute on Aging (NIA), Bethesda, MD.

Research projects: UDS Database (Uniform Data Set), Collaborative research grants, Methodological research grants, involving Alzheimer Disease Centers (ADCs).

Activities: To perform required administrative functions: logistical support for Directors and Core Leaders meetings, interface with NIA 'initiative' groups; provide distribution of funds in support of NACC data collection effort and Collaborative Projects; and inter-ADC communication and other affiliated activities.

Contact information:
- Telephone: (206) 543-8637
- Fax: (206) 616-5927
- E-mail: naccmail@u.Washington.edu
- Website: http://www.alz.Washington.edu/
- Mail address: 4311 11th Ave NE, #300, Seattle, WA 98105, USA

Further reading

Baker M, Mackenzie IR, Pickering-Brown SM, *et al.* (2006). Mutations in progranulin cause tau-negative frontotemporal dementia linked to chromosome 17. *Nature* **442**:916–919.

Chapter 3
Dickson DW (2005). Required techniques and useful molecular markers in the neuropathologic diagnosis of neurodegenerative diseases. [Review] [86 refs] *Acta Neuropathol.* **109**:14–24.

Halliday G, Ng T, Rodriguez M, *et al.* (2002). Consensus neuropathological diagnosis of common dementia syndromes: testing and standardizing the use of multiple diagnostic criteria. *Acta Neuropathol.* 104:72–78.

Knopman DS, Boeve BF, Petersen RC (2003). Essentials of the proper diagnoses of mild cognitive impairment, dementia, and major subtypes of dementia. *Mayo Clin. Proc.* **78**:1290–1308.

Schmitz C, Hof PR (2005). Design-based stereology in neuroscience. [Review] [120 refs] *Neuroscience* **130**:813–831.

Chapter 4
Braak H, Braak E (1997). Frequency of stages of Alzheimer-related lesions in different age categories. *Neurobiol. Aging* **18**:351–357.

Terman A, Brunk UT (2004). Aging as a catabolic malfunction. [Review] [101 refs] *Inter. J. Biochem. Cell Biol.* **236**:2365–2375.

Chapter 5
Petersen RC, Parisi JE, Dickson DW *et al.* (206). Neuropathologic features of amnestic mild cognitive impairment. *Arch. Neurol.* **63**:665–672.

Index